The New Spiritual in Art from Korea – Dàamhua(淡畫) as the Reconfiguring Force of Contemporary Art

Kai Hong,
2003, July

PART I: 'Contemporary Art' as 'the Art After-the-End of Art' as Nihilist Ideology

Prologue: The Problematic of the State of Korean Modernism and/or Postmodernism

I'm going to begin with an apology for the polemical and contentious tone I use, while admitting that it's unusual in a catalogue essay for an Art Institute or a Museum Exhibition such as this one at the famed Institute of Contemporary Art of Singapore. I'm afraid I also need to make another apology for an extended detour which I wish to claim that I am forced to make. What detour? It is that I am writing about the works of Korean Painters represented here at Singapore's ICA exhibition in order to make their works more readily accessible to   the viewers at the exhibition and others who work in the globalized Art Market contexts in all kinds of different capacities. If I wish to make a case for these works as distinct new voices on the global contemporary art scenes, then I'll have to present a different, in fact a radically different characterization of the situation of global Contemporary Art today from the more established and dominant art-discursive frameworks that are usually proffered by the Powers-that-be in the International Market Places of 'Contemporary Art'.

Over the past century or so, the fashionable and dominant critical discourses about Art have all emanated from less than a half-dozen Western centers of culture — in particular New York, London and Paris. This means that the species of art works which are not readily accessible or explainable from within the dominant discursive frameworks of their kinds do have not, do not or perhaps cannot receive fair valuation either from the critics or from the global market forces of International Art. The works of Korean Painters, represented in this Singaporean ICA exhibition, belong to this very species of Art, much more distinct than meets the eye, albeit some familiarity visible in some of them. It is my job to show with some persuasive power that they are and how they are a species of very distinct art, the 'art' quite differently understood from what passes as Art in the global Contemporary Art Scenes everywhere.

For example, these Korean Artists have usually been grouped under the label of 'Korean Monochrome Painting' by the critics based in Korean or in some International Centers of Cultural hegemony in the West for no other reason than that they have been painted in monochrome. For that reason alone, much of what have been written about Korean monochrome painting have been discussed roughly within or against the Western Modernist or Post-Modernist discursive frameworks. But, to place works of these artists in the frame of minimalism, as it's been done, and then to attempt at the understanding of these works in terms of the "formal idioms" and "formal logic" of the New York minimalist aesthetic is tantamount to discounting the value of their works. One of the main purpose of this essay is to address why this is so, as I shall come back to this question again shortly.

In May, 2012, there was a huge --mainly in terms of its sheer size-- exhibition at Korean National Museum of Modern Art, bringing nearly hundred Korean Artists under the banner of '*Dansaekhua*' (which is a literal translation of 'monochrome painting' into Korean)[1]. By itself, the term 'monchrome painting' has no theoretical or historical significance, as it simply refers to a set of all that have been painted in a single color and hue. This term has its use only within the very unique (Western) historical context of modernist discourse. Neither has this term of 'dansaekwa' ever made its appearance among all the art-historical or cultrual-historical writings of East Asia during their history of several millenia. It is simply a conceptually impoverished notion with no explanatory power outside the very specific historical context of Western Modernism. I wish to suggest that it is possible to divide the participating Korean artists at last year's 'dansaekhua' exhibition roughly into two different groups, doing, in fact, mutually incompaitible 'artistic practices'[2].

The first group from that show are actually Monochrome Painters, eganged in 'artistic practices' of Western Painting[3] by the same name, in spite of some ad hoc theorizing as to theirs being distinct artistic production and claiming that their artisic inspiration have been deived from East Asian spiritual resources. Any careful examination of their written claims, however, will reveal that there's no merit to their claims and that their vague references to traditional East Asian spiritual, philosophical and cultural sources are hardly persuasive[4]. It is not unknown that actually a significant portion of practicing Artists and Art College students think that the "main-stream" Art being practiced at the International Centers of the hegemonic West must be the most advanced form of Art and feel that they have to catch up in much the same way an engineering college student might wish to go to one of universities in Silicon Valley or East Coast college towns to study and catch up with the most advanced technologies being invented and practiced at this most advanced (whatever that means), richest   and most powerful nation. Much of the works so ubiquitously visible at any of the so-called 'Contemporary Art' exhibits everywhere today are done by the Artists of such semi-colonial attitudes towards the most developed core countries such as USA and a few Western European countries. Much of their works are, therefore, copy-cat varieties, albeit theirs being, at times, superior than their original from the Western Centers in terms of their technical proficiency and execution. When the nation states of the world are divided into the core and periphery, citizens from the peripheral countries always seem to look towards the dominant Metropolitan Centers of the core nations for inspiration and new ideas. These are important questions to discuss --although not here, however-- as it will mean even further digress. I discuss this issue elsewhere.[5]

Then, there is a much smaller group of painters from the same 2012 Koean National Museum of Modern Art Show of Dansaekhua whose artistic achievements cannot properly be captured by the concept of 'Korean Monochrome Painting." I suggest that these works can be better captured with a new label, other than that of 'dansaekhua,' for the unique kind of Art that they are, intrinsically different from what is today widely accepted as Art in most major international art centers. The new label I wish to christen this body of works with is 'daamhua', composed of two Chinese characters of 'daam'(淡), meaning + 'hua'(畵). This new term, daamhua (淡畵) will be able to capture their distinct artistic practices and philosophy; 'daam'(淡) in 'daamhua'(淡畵) in Korean language has an

[1] Korean National Museum of Modern Art will be referred to as KNMMA from here on.
[2] 'Complex of Practices' is a term Arthur Danto used throughout his book **After the End of Art**, Princeton U Press, 1997
[3] In Korea and Japan, artists are either Western Painting or Oriental Painting. To engage in Western Artistic Practices doesn't mean just that they use Western Material such as Canvas, Oil, Brush, etc; it also means their painting while well aware of the history and tradition of Western Painting, etc.
[4] Such claims have been made most notoriously by Lee Yil, Lee U-huan, Park Yongman, Kim Bokyoung and virtually all other Korean art critics.
[5] It's doubtful if they understand their own East Asian cultural legacies in their genuine terms rather than repeating in formulaic terms what they've learned from those very Centers.

entirely different sort of a meaning from 'dan'(單, meaning mono, single or one) of 'dan-saek-hua'(單色畵). There's a Korean expression: 'Na-neun-daam-daam-hada' which could be translated into English as "I feel calm, at peace, no emotion, having let go of everything –desires, anger, ambition, and so forth. And, now, nothing bothers me." Daam refers to a mood of a human individual.

I believe these Paintings of Daamhua, presented at this Sigaporean ICA Show, not only goes against the grain of the so-called 'Contemporary Art' sensibilities but also promises a way out the nihilistic morass in which 'Contemporary Art' is mired. In order, however, to truly appreciate and perceive the real possibility of their being a radical alternative in Contemporary Art-Practices worldwide, that possibility already present as latent potential in the body of these Paintings from South Korea; a shift in the (theoretical and historical) perspecive, a slight reconfiguring of the established discursive framework of 'Contemporary Art' will be necessay. In other words, of all that have been called Korean Monochrome Paintings, I'll be arguing that only the ones that can be called 'daamhua' paintings are worthy of globe-wide attention, for they promise an altogether distinct and new way of thinking of, on and about art, intrinsically different from what is widely accepted as Art in most global art markets and creative Capitals of the world. In other words, two different groupings are possible of the huge number of Korean Artists whose works were gathered for a massive exhibition under the name of 'Korean Dansaekhua', numbering nearly one hundred artists, each representing different artistic aspirations. The artistry of one of them can be captured by the concept of 'Daamhua' while the other may still be called Korean Monochrome Painting but without authentic and distinct new voice on the horizon of the global art scene. The explanatory account of the concept of 'Daamhua' and historical-contextualizing of its emergence has to wait until later in this essay, as it requires the laying down of a preparatory theoretical groundwork beforehand.

Then, only then, the artistic plentitude and the possibility of a new horizon of art, latent in these works as potential, will become visible, while they remain invisible to those whose viewing practices rely upon the usual dominant discursive frames of contemporary art, being generated for the International Art Establishments ensconced comfortably in the global hub cities –the International Centers of cultural hegemony. For that purpose, I wish to contest the most influential theories (story-telling) of the *End of Art* theories and of the Art after the End of Art, especially the ones provided by Arthur Danto, who probably has the reputation of being the finest philosopher of history and of art in the academic world of Anglo-american Analytic Philosophy.

Contemporary Art defined in 'the End of Art' Discourses: Danto, Belting, etc.

Just as the globalization of what can basically be said to be American Form of Life have profoundly transformed the way people live in every corner of this world, making the urbanized landscapes of nearly all the countries look the same and peoples in them living a similar forms of consumers' lives; there's been a globalization of the Art Worlds as well, showing pretty much similar kinds of the so-called 'Contemporary Art' in the galleries and museums in all those similarly planned and built urban centers of the world, whether it be in Seoul, Korea, Singapore, Tokyo, Paris, London, New York, Beijing, Shanghai or Berlin. This is indeed very surprising in view of the fact that they all mouth 'diversity' and 'multiculturalism'.

What is this globalized Art called 'Contemporary Art' in one great globalized Art World (with globalized Art Market)? As always, it is defined by a variety of basically similar discourses generated from the International Art and Cultural Centers – it'd be better to call 'art-cultural hegemonic centers of the world, most prominently from New York, the power center not only of the arts but also of global finance, mass media and marketing (general consumer products, political candidates, ideologies of and for all sorts of different things, art and religion and whatever else). Arthur Danto, the distinguished Professor of Philosophy at Columbia and the in-house art critic for one of the most prestigious Journal of 'Nation', says that 'contemporary' in the phrase 'Contemporary Art' is not "merely a temporal concept, meaning whatever is taking place at the present moment" and that "shift from modern to contemporary art" is as momentous a change as the shift from '*pre-modern* ' to modern was.[6]

As such, his definition of Contemporary Art is all kinds of different varieties of the Arts that came after the Death of Art, more specifically after the demise of Modern Art. We can see what he means by observing the way he differentiates his version of the End of Art from another influential account given by New York Critic, Douglas Crimp: for example, while Crimp's version is based on the judgment that "advanced painting seemed to show all the signs of internal exhaustion, or at least marked limits beyond which it was not possible to press," his and Belting's versions implies "that art should be very vigorous and show no sign whatever of internal exhaustion" at the end point of art.[7] Thus, for Danto and Belting, the end of art does not mean the exhaustion or the actual death of art as such, but, on the contrary, merely that "one complex of (art) practices had given way to another, even if the shape of the new complex was still unclear."[8] Here, Danto means by "complex of practices" something very much like Kuhn's scientific paradigm, as is evident from his reference to the Vassarian representational master narrative, given its initial articulation during the Quatrocento but became exhausted (after going through many slight variations on the same theme) at the point of the advent of the Modernity and to be followed by the master narrative of modernism, the most definitive articulation of which was given by Clement Greenberg, with which he single-handedly helped give New York the moniker of being THE International Center of global Arts and Culture, taking away that status long held by Paris (or London or Berlin or Vienna as other sometime pretenders).

The master narrative of modernism a la Greenberg exhausted its usefulness by the 1960s in the shape of Monochrome Paintings of Ad Reinhart or Ryman or Stella's Shaped canvases, but according to Danto it was not the End of Art as such, but only that *Art-ing* (or doing-art) began to be done in an altogether different Complex (or Paradigm) of artistic practices (*henceforth it'll be referred as 'Art-ing'*) will be practiced with even greater vigor and life, as evidenced by the flourishing, globalized Art Markets as never before in history (having become an International Industry with strong financial components). Notice that the key notions of 'mass', 'energy' and 'force' do not preserve their meaning across the paradigmatic shift from Newtonian Classical Mechanics to the Relativistic Mechanics a la Einstein, even while they're expressed in the very same English words. Likewise, for Danto, even the very concepts of Art or works of art changes their meaning in the "Complex of Artistic Practices" in the name of 'Contemporary Art', which he also calls by the name of Post-Historical Art or the Art 'after the End of Art', or equivalently "Post-Modern" Art. It will be shown to be important to take notice that in Danto's version of the new paradigm of Contemporary Art, it doesn't matter how some of the practices of *Art-ing* after the end of modernism are called, whether in the name of 'neo-avant-garde', 'pop', 'minimalism', 'postmodernism', 'art povera' or 'dematerialized art' or whatever else. For, what characterizes the situation of contemporary art is the sheer pluralism and "any and everything goes!"

One might be easily misled when he or she comes across a piece of art-writing such as this one by Hal Foster: "Such paradigms as 'the neo-avant-garde' and 'postmodernism', which once oriented some art and theory, have run into the sand, and, arguably, no models of much explanatory reach or

[6] Danto, <u>After the End of Art</u>, p.9~10;
[7] Danto, p.4. ibid.
[8] Danto, op cited.

intellectual force have risen in their stead," while at the same time, "'contemporary art' has become an institutional object in its own right."[9] One might think from these quotes that 'postmodernism' or 'the neo-avant-garde' was the succeeding paradigms at the end point of the modernist paradigm's reign. Of course, only in retrospect at the vantage point of 2010, the once fashionable discourses of 'postmodernism' or 'the neo-avant-garde' or other bunch of such ad hoc flimsy discourses have all proven to be nothing but just a lot of noise, Foster seems to admit. To admit that only in retrospect, could he come belatedly to ask this question of "Is this floating-free real or imagined?", however, belies some very important set of unjustified beliefs (of ideological kinds) that the influential 'postmodern' art-theorists and critics such as Hal Foster himself had to bring to their conceptualization of 'art', 'art practices', 'art history' and the nature of writing about art, etc. Two of the most crucial such assumptions, unvoiced, are first that it is their (the likes of Foster, Danto and others') unswerving conviction that whatever happens in the Western Centers (in New York after WWII) is the most *advanced* in whatever field of the Arts, Sciences, Technologies, Political Thinking and what have you. Just notice how casually, without any justification, nay without any thought that the use of the words, "the most advanced art", might require at least some justification, in the writings of both Danto and Hal Foster.[10] Secondly, especially in the case of Foster, by coming to ask that question of the state of contemporary art belatedly, is to have failed to notice the sheer historical importance of the failure of Greenbergian articulation of the Modernist master narrative. (It is not enough to take note of it; it is critically important to understand why and how it failed.) It should also be noticed that there is a distinct possibility that Foster and Danto and all the rest of the supposedly most brilliant and astute art-theorists of the Western hegemonic Centers might have chosen, possibly, very possibly *willfully* to ignore that there might be some other, possibly more persuasive account of modernism than Greenberg's and also that they all failed to give coherent explanatory accounts for two of the most critical art-historical events of the past one hundred years – namely, of the failure of Greenberg's modernist master narrative and of *L'affaire Duchamp*. That choice, perhaps not consciously, I claim, must have been ideologically motivated; otherwise, it's mystifying how such brilliant intellects could have turn blind eyes to other potentially more persuasive narrative account (or simply the 'story-telling') of how Western Art have come to an End and to the very unviable state of nihilism for the 'Western Art(s) After the Rain,' as it were. Let me explain:

Politics of Writing about Art, especially of 'Contemporary' Art

For a Philosopher of History (of course, he is better known as a Professor of Philosophy of Art and New York Art Critic for the prestigious magazine NATION), Danto is near-sighted in that he, too assiduously following Hans Belting the German Art Historian, in going only back to the 14th Century ('Quattro-Cento') of Vasari's time in his Kuhnian historiographical sketch of the Western Art History, claiming that the era of art began only then; previous to that era of Quattrocento, there was no human practice under the name of 'Art'. It is strange that Danto fell for the German Art Historian's pedantry of rejecting all previous era as having not produced any sort of Art on a purely ad hoc patched-up reasoning of pedantry. I mean, are we not willing to call the ancient Greek temples and sculpture Art –in fact, great Arts? How about 11th Century Sung Period Chinese masterpieces such as Fan K'uan's and Kuo Hsi's massive 'Mountains and River' Paintings? It is for this nearsightedness that Danto and Belting, not to speak of lesser eminent scholars and art-critical theorists of faultless reputation, failed and still fails to persuasively characterize the state of Art today on a global scale. I suggest that there's a much more persuasive (and also consonant with the

---

[9] Hal Foster, "Contemporary Extracts", e-flux journal #1-- January 2010

[10] Danto, After the End of Art, op cited; See also Hal Foster, "Dan Flavin and the Catastrophe of Minimalism."

historical realities) account of the Death of Art and the dire crisis of Contemporary Art (however it is defined) than the ones given by Arthur Danto and other influential art critics and scholars at the hegemonic centers ('hegemonic' in the sense of Immanuel Wallerstein's World-Systems theory) of the Western World, especially New York – Oh, the New York, New York, indeed!

In contradistinction to Danto's account, Martin Heidegger gives us another Philosophy of History superior to Danto's Hegel in understanding the current dire situation of Contemporary Art. For Heidegger, the dire situation of Contemporary Art is not unrelated to the crisis of the technologically configured global world system of today-- crisis at all levels from its very material foundation to its superstructure; it is one of rare historical states of anomie precipitated by the (metaphysical) 'closure'. Even though, strictly speaking, this 'closure' refers to the West, the rest of the world also have to encounter and deal with this 'closure', having been kidnapped, as it were, by the West and forced into sharing what should be the West's historical destiny. In such a time, only in such a time, is it possible for 'men' to *engage*[11] in 'epochal thinking' à la Heidegger; only at the point of closure, is it possible to go all the way back to the point of its very 'beginning' (origin) for an 'originative thinking'. It is none other than the historical deconstruction of the entire stretch of the metaphysical tradition of the West from Plato to Nietzsche, the very last Metaphysician, as Heidegger famously put. The critical procedure of historical deconstruction is to rigorously interrogate important key concepts of that particular way of thinking by tracing all the way back to their originary sources in order hopefully to restructure or re-configure (Western) modern civilization for a new foundation.

Metaphysical Closure thus implies not only *the end of philosophy* for Heidegger but also for *the end of art* as well, as is evident in his comments on Hegel's Aesthetics – 'the most comprehensive meditation on art the West possesses, because it is 'conceived on the basis of the whole of metaphysics' – and his conclusion on the death of art. On this point, both of the American (analytic) Philosopher, Arthur Danto and a distinguished German Art Historian Hans Belting agree with Heidegger in according the utmost seriousness to Hegel's verdict on the state of Art –namely, its end. Taking Hegel's Phenomenology of Spirit as the master narrative of the Geist (or the' World Spirit') in its developmental unfolding with its eventual Ending as the latent potentiality of the Geist (from the very beginning) and this Ending for Danto also means the Death of the Master Narrative a la Hegel. As with the master narrative of the Geist, so is with the Master Narrative of the Western traditional Art as well as the Modern Art. The Death of Western Art is actually the death of Clement Greenberg's master narrative of Modernism. Danto looks upon the latency of the Geist's potentiality (i.e., the developmental possibilities) and the consequent exhaustion and demise (the no-longer viable) with which the inevitable putting down of the story-telling—namely, the end of that master narrative, which can no longer be continued. In some such ways, Danto has taken over the Hegelian model for his own explanatory account of the historical 'End of Art'.

If Hegelian Master narrative was the story of the historical destiny of the World Spirit as it progressively unfolded, it is the historical destiny not of the World Art but of the limited (and expected) historical life-time of the Vassarian master narrative of the Western traditional Representational Painting and also its immediate successor, Greenbergian master narrative of modernism that were the thematic of this "End of Art" discourses. I came back to this point, risking repetitiveness, to call attention that Danto and Belting's appropriation of Hegelian model is only partial. It is to me quite extraordinary to me that this scholar of very highest reputation in the academic world of the so-called Anglo-American Analytic Philosophy is intellectually posturing

---

[11] For Lacoue-Labarth, such a thinking is demanded by the Age at such a time of a Metaphysical Closure in his Heidegger, Art and Politics; it is also called 'Epochal Principle' by Reiner Schürmann in Heidegger on Being and Acting: From Principles to Anarchy,p.112.

here, not unlike some Art-School types of some historical or neo-avant-garde pretensions. It is his Hegelian posturing, I have in mind here. For example, he initially called the Art after the End of Art as "Post-Historical Art", which also brings to our mind once fashionable thesis put forward in a book called End of History, fashionable through noise marketing in the industrialized academia in the name of Education-Industry, especially in the United States and faithfully copied by Japan, Korea and other developing and developed countries, co-opted into the Free (-wheeling) Market System.

Unlike Heidegger, they do not look all the way back to the originary sources of Western thinking (thinking about art is a part and parcel of it, in fact an integral part of it), going back only to the 14th Century. I wish to show before I end this essay that this seemingly small difference matters a great deal and also how the most influential generators of art-discourses on Contemporary Art from the International Centers of Art and Culture of the hegemonic West have, possibly, very possibly, suppressed the emergence of any sort of equally persuasive but challenging explanatory accounts of the nature and situation of Contemporary Art, while turning blind eyes to the very possibility of such in a kind of political-ideological choice. This applies not only to Danto and Belting but all the other intellectual eminences of the Western Academic-Journalistic-Art Market-Cultural Complex (not much different from the better known Military-Industrial-Academic Complex), whether it's Fried, Krauss, Foster, Urlrich, Agamben or whoever else.

Danto acknowledges that others, most prominently Douglas Crimp had also come up with the idea of the End of Art somewhat earlier or roughly at the same time as he, but wishes to point out that Crimp's account was based on his judgment that "advanced painting seemed to show all the signs of internal exhaustion, or at least marked limits beyond which it was not possible to press."[12] The critical weakness of Crimp's account of the death of art is that it fails to explain the extreme vigor of art, with no signs of internal exhaustion, after the end of art. In contradistinction, his and Belting's proposal for the end of art had nothing to do with actual *death* of art; rather, "ours was a claim about how one complex of practices had given way to another, even if the shape of the new complex was still unclear –is still unclear."[13]

It is clear that Danto and Belting views the end of art as really **only** an end of the modernist paradigm of art which has been replaced by a new paradigm that can be called 'Art after the End of Art' or more commonly called in global art markets as 'Contemporary Art'.[14] "As the history of art has internally evolved, contemporary has come to mean an art produced within a certain structure of production never, I think, seen before in the entire history of art." What characterizes the situation of Art after the End of Art (sic Contemporary Art), according to Danto is that "there really are no rules, it remains an open possibility that artists might pursue the art of painting in whatever way they care to, and under whatever imperatives they may care to work –it is only that those imperatives are *no longer grounded in history*" and that "accommodation is the key to survival in *an art world in which everything goes.*"[15]

An Alternative Characterization: the Situation of Contemporary Art

I suggest that Danto's, Greenberg's, Beltings', and other widely accepted understandings of Modernism in the history of Western Art are in error in thinking that Modernism denotes an entirely new Socio-Cultural Convention of Modernist Painting. Notice that I choose to use the term 'socio-cultural convention' rather than 'paradigm' à la Foster or 'complex of practices' à la Danto. While a

---

[12] P.4 Danto, After the End of Art;
[13] P.4, Danto, ibid.,
[14] P.10, Danto ibid
[15] P.172, Danto, ibid

socio-cultural convention in fact denotes a way of life pretty much in the same sense of the notion of the "Form of Life" as in Wittgenstein's "language is a form of life", Danto's 'complex' or Foster's 'paradigm' denotes a kind of 'complex of practices in a profession' as in Kuhn's sense of the term 'paradigm'. (In fact, I argue elsewhere that art is just like language every human being is born with an innate knowledge of universal grammar, nothing less.) Only when we understand the notion of art, in some intrinsic way, as an aspect of the 'Form of Life', is it possible to propose the following kind of story-telling concerning the sorely tangled and difficult concept of modernism or postmodernism, made even worse by the utterly irresponsible and insincere 'anything goes' variety of theorizing of the past three or four decades in the artistic and intellectual centers of Western hegemony. Let me explain:

The historical process of modernization via rationalization had its enemies from within –namely, the unforeseen consequences that were unacceptable. Max Weber famously put the problems of modernization via rationalization in a short terse phraseology: 'Paradox of Modernity' or the 'Predicament of Modernity.' He pointed out that modernization via rationalization of all productive processes in human affairs would end up putting the very Subjects (the subject-agents of rationalization) in 'iron cages', spiritually diminished instead of enhancing their *spiritual freedom* as Hegel thought the final stage of the History of the World Spirit would bring about, as its final realization.

Modernism is nothing other than the taking seriously of the historically immanent situation of modernity's paradox and thinking through the dire situation of the predicament of modernity in order to find a way out, if at all possible. This predicament of modernity shows up in the arts (whether it is in musical composition, painting or literature or theatre) in the following way: Sometime in the middle of the 19th Century, advanced composers and artists began to feel that the traditional convention of their respective realm of art had been broken down and couldn't go on in the same old ways to do their arts[16]. This is a crisis in fact, because *Art-ing* is by its very nature social, much the same way any sort of language behavior is social; and therefore *Art-ing* (doing-art) cannot be done in the absence of a set of accepted (in common) rules of grammar, just as no one can speak a language without mastering its grammatical rules. This fact is implied in Wittgenstein's famous thesis of the "Impossibility of Private Language."

The question, then, is this: how to go on in the absence of an implicitly agreed-upon socio-cultural convention of *'Art-ing'*, as a species of social act. In the conception of modernism à la Danto et al of the West, it might just be the breaking-down of Vassarian paradigm merely to be replaced by another paradigm of modernism. For Heidegger, contrary to theirs, it is not merely the breaking down of Vassarian convention of only several hundred years, but is the result of the 'Metaphysical Closure' of *the entire stretch* of Western tradition after more than two thousand years' running, from Plato of Ancient Greece to Nietzsche, the Last Metaphysician, roughly, at the middle of the 19th Century. Only then, only at such a point of a grand 'closure', is a thinking with Epochal Principle possible, which is actually none other than the historical deconstruction of interrogating, retrospectively, the entire stretch of Western History back to its originary sources. Modernist Painting (the master narrative of which had been given best articulation by Greenberg, in Danto's assessment, for example), then, would be the only option left for any serious minded advanced Artists, be they a composer, painter or a writer, to do at such a point –i.e., to pursue "Art for Art's Sake." What do I mean by a modernist option?

In such a dire condition of having suddenly lost a language of art, it is either to stop to do art or to ask how this situation came about and then start asking fundamental questions about their very

---

[16] Stanley Cavell, "Music Discomposed" in MUST WE MEAN WHAT WE SAY?, p.186

Arting practices by way of interrogating the tradition he or she had inherited: in other words, begin to do historical deconstruction of the traditional mimetic convention of painting from the time of Plato on down to the time of Nietzsche, the last Western Metaphysician, at roughly the middle of the 19th Century.

Although Clement Greenberg was not able to see what they were actually doing in the short history of Modernist Painting from Edvard Manet (Middle of the 18th Century) on down to Frank Stella (Stella's first Shaped Canvas Series of the early 1960s), theirs was a historically deconstructive painting, peeling off layer after layers of the more two millennia long mimetic tradition of Western Art; his sensitive minutely detailed description of what the Modernist Painters were doing was correct and unsurpassable. It is only that these painters were not through their works establishing any sort of new socio-cultural convention of painting, a new language of art, initiating an entirely new tradition of art for Western Painting. While they were dealing with the Modernist Problematic –the Predicament of Modernity which showed up as the breakdown of their inherited traditional convention of Painting, they were seemingly able to prolong the Life of Western Painting, however tenuous. Their painterly meditation, however, was done still in terms of the idioms from their inherited tradition, even while rejecting and disowning that very tradition. To make better sense of what I mean, just consider what modernist composers did in the same situation as the Modernist Painters found themselves in: they came up with an idea of *a-tonal* music. But a-tonal music made sense only vis-à-vis the language of tonal music, as a-tonal music was not a language in its own right, entirely dependent on the tonal convention for its semantic efficacy. In so far as these modernist painters were doing historically deconstructive (while they were not consciously aware) painting from within the traditional convention, they were not coming up with any sort of a new language of art at all.

Historically Deconstructive Painting and Musical Composition:

With the language in crisis, when in terms of whose idioms it is no longer possible to speak a language and then be understood in genuine terms, those idioms having become mere clichés; then, Language as the "house of Being" à la **Heidegger** or as the "Form of Life" à la Wittgenstein is no longer that. Language is in crisis as the great Linguist Noam Chomsky also points out; it is left with a mere shell, its reserve of the spiritual and creative resources depleted, and has become a mere source code book for mechanical speaking in formulae for technical purposes of a mere consuming life of all different kinds of *industrial* **products**[17] in late Capitalist World of an American version or 'Americanism' in Heidegger's coinage[18].

Stanley Cavell's diagnosis on the same situation of modernism was this: "What characterizes the situation in modern arts (in the West) today is the pervasive possibility of fraudulence."[19] This is a semantically compacted statement, to its extremity, and requires unpacking. In the absence of a

---

[17] Here 'industrial products' do not denote only the industrial goods, but also food, intellectual and spiritual products as well. It is so, insofar as these are produced for mass consumption en masse. For example, music industry, Hollywood films, etc. Having every sector human form of life having become industrialized, whether it is a farm industry, fashion industry, medical industry, and education industry, financial industry, or culture industry, content industry, so on and on. There's art industry too; how else can you explain the phenomenon of Damien Hearst? Sachi and Sachi's marking of the Dead Shark in a Glass Box? It was done as an entrepreneurial project, because they saw the possibility of marketing, a niche market, perhaps, but nevertheless a market.

[18] Heidegger on "Americanism" is quoted by M.Zimmerman, **Heidegger's Confrontation with Modernity: Technology, Politics, Art**, p.41, 42, Heidegger's equation of Americanism with Bolshevism, p.90, 264-265;

[19] Stanley Cavell, "Music Discomposed" in Must We Mean What We Say?

language (a convention), there's no grammatical criteria for distinguishing grammatical sentences from the ungrammatical, art from non-art. If someone does any stupid thing and calls it art, there's no criterion by which to say that it is not. Even it what one does in the name is not prima facie stupid, making some sense at least in the way he or she explains what's been done in the art; it is not possible to accord it 'art', as there's no criterion by which to assent to the claim of 'art'. It is in some such ways a dire situation, a "Crisis of Language" à la Chomsky, whereby no one can, in good conscience or in good faith, claim to be *art-ing* (doing-art). Since no one claim to be doing art in good faith, whatever is done in the name of art is fraudulent. (Isn't what is done in bad faith the hall-mark of fraudulence?)

For Danto, it seems like to be saying, in such a situation, anything can be done in the name of art and it is art. Instead of despairing at such a situation, it is something to be celebrated. To him, it [the 'anything does', 'everything goes'] opens up the possibility of a great new future of everything, be it art, politics, economy or what have you, a new global culture, embracing multiculturalism, multiracialism, multi-this, multi-that, rejoicing in the sheer plurality –"the deep structure is a kind of unprecedented pluralism"[20]. I agree with Danto –at least one this thing-- when he claims that many Post-Modernist art critics, in giving what was and is fashionable "deconstructionist account," failed "to go to the heart of the matter –to what I want to think of as the deep structure of art history in the contemporary era." However, Danto fails to make a distinction between Heidegger's "historical deconstruction" and the French version of pseudo deconstruction (plagiarizing from Heidegger).

Francophile deconstructionist might not have gone deep enough to see the deep structure of Post-Historical Contemporary art, but the historical deconstruction in epochal thinking à la Heidegger goes even deeper and find Danto's deep structure wanting. To have seen "pluralism" in his sense of "anything goes" is to have seen nothing much. What he should have seen is *nihilism* of merely playing an endless end-game with no exit in sight. What is he afraid of? Why not call it by its right name? This question can be posed to both Cavell and Danto and other influential art theorists of the Western hegemonic Centers. So, then, are they not in fact secretly the cultural apologists, devising all kinds of ad hoc, patched up theories, discourses, in order to preserve the dominance of *the* hegemonic powers-that-be of today whose dominance reaches into every single sector of the public life of 'global village' which this planet earth has become. Yes, in that world in which 'junk bonds' are transformed into "hedge funds", creating shark waves over the globalized financial world, while producing nothing to enhance human life but merely to create further newer fashions of "products of financial industry" for mass marketing and instant huge profits; Pieces of Garbage are turned into Multimillion Dollar Art Work to market in today's art market (cum fund market).

Misreading of L'affaire Duchamp & Warholian Pop: Ideologically Motivated?

Both Danto and Hal Foster look to Duchamp for having opened up an entire new horizon of *arting*, the new avant-garde art of 'anything goes', having inspired John Cage in Music, and, according to Danto, also the now famous America's invention –namely, the Pop Art of Andy Warhol. For Danto, Warhol's *Brillo Hat* (purchased from a shop, a species of mass factory-produced ready-made consumer product, presented as a work of art) is just what Duchamp did with his Urinal. Duchamp and Warhol ushered in a new Convention of *Arting* (or a 'new paradigm' of doing-art), now all the terms in the previous convention of doing art have taken on differently changed meanings, even though they are denoted by the same words like 'art' or 'exhibition' or 'work of art' and other such.

---

[20] Danto, After the End of Art, p.

But Duchamp's gesture of presenting an industrially produced Urinal in an Gallery Exhibition can be given an entirely different interpretation; and an entirely different historical narrative of the so-called Post-Modern or Post-historical or new Avant-garde Arts (in whatever different versions and names) can also be constructed with equally plausible story-telling as the ones so far provided by such famous art critics as Rosalind Krauss, Arthur Danto, Hal Foster, David Crimp or whoever else equally famous and pretty much accepted as the standard narratives by the Powers-that-be in Today's Globalized Art World(s).

An entirely different interpretation of Duchampian gesture can be given, by, for example, taking an early article by Ted Cohen, the University of Chicago Philosopher of Art titled "The Possibility of Art", in which he demonstrated that Duchamp's wasn't himself intending the exhibited Urinal in a Paris Gallery actually to be taken as a Work of Art as such; instead, his sole intention was to make a point and raise a question about the State of Art in Western Art by *calling attention to the very act or gesture of so doing*. **Art-ing**[21] is a social act just like any linguistic act (or speech act) of speaking a language is. As such, any speech act must satisfy some implicitly agreed upon social convention before it can be accepted as that social act, having the right kinds of social consequence in that language community –yes, indeed, again the famous Wittgenstein's thesis that "to imagine a language is to imagine a form of life." In analogy to speech acts as social acts in a real community of people, so **Arting** as a social act must satisfy a set of implicitly agreed upon conditions before it can be accepted as **Arting**. But that doesn't mean sometimes some speech acts, although not acceptable as a socially efficacious act, can nevertheless be taken as meaningful act.

Ted Cohen gives an example of the speech act of 'promising'. "I promise to love you forever" is a grammatical English sentence and any native speaker would understand the meaning of this sentence. However, it fails to be a social act of promising in uttering that sentence. For it fails to satisfy the condition of good faith to actually to keep the promise; it not it would then be a false promise. So this sentence is not a social act of promising, as that promise cannot be kept, as no human-being is capable of living forever to keep the promise. Still, this sentence is not meaningless. It can be construed as an act of exclamation of a sort in the sense of simply that "I love you very, very much." It was uttered in order to call attention of others to this very act of saying this very thing. Likewise, Duchamp's presenting an industrially produced Urinal as a work of art in an art exhibition at a gallery should be understood as a singular gesture of calling attention of others to that very gesture itself, thus making the viewer at the gallery to think and to question about the very notion of a "Work of Art." There's no good reason to think that Duchamp was conferring a new ontological status of a "Work of Art" to an industrially produced ready-made in his gesture. Notice, in fact, that Duchamp never repeated that same gesture, stopping to do art henceforth; he was right to do so, because his was a singular gesture which cannot be repeated, having raised the question that he wanted to ask in the first place.

In other words, he was raising questions, the question about the still-persisting institutional practices of the then Art World of Paris at that time, blithely ignoring the dire Condition of Western Art. So, if the Modernist Painting was a self-reflexive interrogation of their inherited traditional convention of painting *from within* in an act of historical deconstruction; then, the Duchampian gestures were a species of guerrilla warfare against (**vis-à-vis** the still-persisting traditional institutional practices of Art World in all hypocrisies from *the outside.(from without)*. So, the very

---

[21] I prefer this, instead of the usual 'doing-art' or 'art-practice' for the way it sounds, immediately bringing to one's mind another English word, 'farting', which in fact captures what the fashionable contemporary artists, Stars at the influenza-area called 'International Art Bienales do as Nihilist 'Guhndahls' en Correan.

gesture of Duchampian kind does indeed belong to the history of modern art but not as a bona-fide Work of Art. That means, such gestures cannot be given either repeat performances or repeat exhibitions, as *that* question has been raised in that particular gesturing and has been taken note of, period. Performance Arts are species of allographic Art in Nelson Goodman's terminology, requiring a *score* before there can be repeat performances by the same artist or by others (of the same score). John Cage's famous Piano piece called "Silence for 4minutes and 33 seconds" is a species of Duchampian gesture and as such it cannot be given repeat performances. Nor can Nam Jun Paik give repeat performances of smashing a Piano or Violin at different occasions. That they do indicate neither Cage nor Paik have understood the true meaning of the Duchmpian gesture. (Yes, incredibly, there're, some people, self-proclaimed 'Art-Theorists, have' quoted Ted Cohen's paper as if Cohen's analysis of Duchampian gesture on the basis of Speech Act Theory had given them the conceptual legitimacy to upgrade the ontological status of Duchampian 'Ready-mades' into the class of 'Works of Art'. I believe that's a misreading of Cohen paper. Interesting to notice what a mental fixation can do in the name of conceptual clarification of 'Avant-garde' Art.) Isn't it interesting to notice that the neo-avant-garde paradigm had been built on theoretical sand--on a serious intellectual failure of misunderstanding *L'affaire Duchamp*?[22]

If Clement Greenberg was the greatest theoretician and advocate of Abstract Expressionism, it was Arthur Danto who is the greatest theorizer and advocate of Pop Art. Notice the effusively celebratory remarks made by Danto on Pop Art such as the following:

> "*Pop art as such consists in what I term transfiguring emblems from popular culture into high art. It requires recreating the logo as socialist realist art, or making the Campbell's soup can the subject of a genuine of oil painting which uses commercial art as a painterly style. Pop art was so exciting because it was transfigurative.*

> "*Pop art as such was a properly American achievement, and I think it was the transfigurativeness of its basic stance that made it so subversive abroad.*" (p.128)

> "*Analytic Philosophy set itself against the whole of philosophy, from Plato through Heidegger. Pop set itself against art as a whole in favor of real life.*" (pp.130~131)[23]

Any Warhol's very first pop version of art made its first appearance in 1964 when he displayed a Brillio Hat, just picked up from some Supermarket. Later, he would pick just any consumer products such as Campbell Soup Cans as his subject for representational oil painting or silk-screening. So, what might be the difference between Dumchamp's 1915 presentation of Industrial Ready-made in an art show and Warhol's Brillio Hat? While I cannot go into it in this essay[24], as it will take me too far off, let me just state that I disagree with Danto that their gestures (of Duchamp and Warhol) are different in kind. A radical difference, I too see in the two, but something Danto doesn't see or possibly willfully ignoring, while he also sees it? Well, Danto himself quotes Wittgenstein's famous "language" as "form of life" in order to press the point that art is unhinged when it is alienated from the contexts of real life, ordinary life. Danto celebrates the fact the Pop Artists take anything from ordinary life's contexts and pop culture and transfigure them into Art of High Culture through a variety of creative and technical means.

---

[22] It is heartening to see Hal Foster admitting as much in his rueful reminiscence: "neo-avant-garde, postmodernism, etc, they all ran into sand." in e-flux journal #12 –Jan.2010, **Contemporary Extracts.**
[23] Danto, After the End of Art, op cited.
[24] I will give an extended argument on this point in a separate paper to be published elsewhere.

But let us ask what form of life can we imagine when we consider works of Pop Art? Is it not American style of Consumption Culture of everything industrially mass produced? Life, every aspect of ordinary life, has been overtaken by Industrial Processes as we can easily see in the increasingly proliferating new industries –power industry, oil industry, manufacturing industry, farm industry, food industry, education industry, finance industry, fashion industry, hotel industry, construction industry, urban-planning Corporation, or whatever else. Is there any human endeavor that has not been taken over by industrialization? No wonder that 'management science' is the finest invention of American genius. Pop Art celebrates this life.

In the decades of the 60s and 70s, Pop art was subversive, for American style of "living an industrialized life" was destructive of more traditional societies of other Continents. No wonder that Paul Ricoeur raised this poignant question[25]: (in my own paraphrase) No nation and people can safely reject what seems to be the universal historical process of modernization (via industrialization) and however is it possible to modernize and yet not also completely Americanized, by preserving at least a modicum of the very essence of their spiritual and cultural legacies? For Danto, it might be something to celebrate, this celebration of artificial, industrialized way of life of America; but Heidegger it was the greatest danger facing the humanity –the inexorable spread of Americanism. Noam Chomsky too, in my reading, shares with Heidegger that the dominance of American hegemonic power spills over into all other areas of human life other than the usual economic, financial and political dominance. Unlike Warhol, Duchamp was not celebrating the post-modern culture (or the Contemporary Culture in Danto and Hal Foster's understandings of the term) of "anything goes".

The Post-historical ideology of "anything goes" is basically this: Each and everything of all kinds (material, spiritual, intellectual, or cultural or whatever else) under the sky and on the earth is, from within that cultural calculus, turned into arithmetical number in dollar units and then play around with different statistical or mathematical models, letting them go through further and further mathematical transformations, for no reason than that it can be done in order create new fashion and newer fashion for consumption of automobiles, foods, cultures high and low, even moral values, life style, . . . Is this not *Nihilism of Playing an endless end-game on and on, unable to get out that morass?* The difference between Duchamp and Warhol might be that one is a European and the latter an American, reveling in the riches of all the junk produces to consume and relish. Notice that the ascendency of Pop Art coincides with the inchoate Food and Farm Industry. At the time, Food industry turning out frozen foods, canned foods, fast foods were celebrated, as the transformative agent for making ordinary home life easier, more convenient, and healthful. I'd like to ask Professor Danto if those promises of Pop Culture of fast food, canned culture, etc. lived up to its original promises or not; on the contrary, now we know that the food industry and farm industry have been the culprits of debilitating chronic illnesses of the population. If fast food proved to be no good for anyone's healthful living; will fast cultural products as canned cultural contents (the products of music industry, video and online game industries, etc.) prove to be equally detrimental or not?

Let me conclude the first part of this essay with a brief resume. Well, yes, it is sort of true that what has been going on in the so-called International Centers of Global Art World such as New York or Paris in the name of Art cannot simply be dismissed as non-art; the reason is there's no longer any sort of *shared convention of doing-art and therefore there cannot be a clear set of criteria (which can be derived or discovered only from within a shared convention) for distinguishing art from non-art.* But, then, *fortiori*, neither can they legitimize what they do in the name of 'Post-Modern Art' or

---

[25] Paul Ricoeur, "Universal Civilization and National Cultures", in History and Truth, pp.276-7; He doesn't use the word 'Americanization', but that's what he means in the context of his extended argument there.

of 'Post-Historical Art' (of 'anything goes') **as Art** in good conscience, in good faith. It won't do simply to say, "Well, we are doing art in differently understood sense of the term, Art." Well, really? Do we need a Child to call things by their right names in today's art world? What passes as Art in today's Art World is nothing other than nihilistic posturing and gesturing of non-sense and vacuity. Global Art World is just like the 'virtual world' of Financial Engineering or technology of Wall Street (NYC) or the City of London where they turn any collection of worthless junk bonds into *'Hedge Funds'* after some series of phase transformations of variously different mathematical and/or statistical models. Voila, the Alchemy of transforming junk bonds into Gold Bars, so to speak.

Is there a possibility of finding an exit from this endless end-game in the so-called "most advanced art" of the global art world? Surely, the crisis of the global Art World is intimately connected to the dire situation of the humanity (as well as other phenomena of life on this planet) in which their very survival qua spiritual beings is in question, all because we're living in a technologically-configured Modern Civilization. As the crisis of Modern Civilization has its intellectual **root-cause** in its Representational Thinking; so did the crisis of Art in the breakdown of the traditional convention of doing-art had its **root-cause** in its Representational Seeing of the external world as objects (passively there in objectified nature, helplessly as it were) at the disposal of the seeing eyes of the Subject, the aggressive focusing of his eye-sight being controlled by his unconscious desires buried deep underneath the surface of his consciousness. Then, must we not ask this question: is it at all possible to imagine a thinking that is nonrepresentational and an Art, a conception of Art (and of Painting as well) which is not premised upon a representational seeing or eye-sight? Unfortunately, such thinking and such a seeing cannot be imagined from within Occidental Ways of seeing, thinking and doing.

Such was the conclusion that Martin Heidegger, perhaps one of the two or three Greatest Philosophers who have ever lived in history, drew. He despaired at the possibility of a way out of the looming crisis of Man (qua spiritual being) from the morass of Nihilism which is another name for the Religion of Technological Faith, the unshakable faith that there are technological solutions to anything, any questions, any problems of any kinds, mattering not whether it's a moral, political, aesthetic, psychological, social, spiritual or medical problem. It's a Religion of Technopia of which both Americans (Capitalists) and the former Soviet Bolsheviks (the Marx-Leninists) were equally devout faithful followers. (Heidegger saw no difference between Americanism and Bolshevism, both being worshipers at the dais of Technopia.[26] Notice that with God dead, Men, at least some men began to simulate the Omnipotence of God himself in, for example, inventing and actually using Atom Bomb and thus demonstrating Man's Power to destroy the entire world with his own concoction –namely, that is in fact a Power to match the God's. Only God, we thought until then, could create and destroy the entire World. At least for Destructive purposes, Man has equaled God's Power.

The Western kind of Representational Thinking did initiate and create Western Civilization as we know it today; Well, Martin Heidegger interrogated the nature of Western Thinking entirely *from within* Western Tradition, forward and backward from PLATO to Nietzsche, and despaired at finding a way out of the morass of the crisis of Western Civilization; furthermore, he couldn't find an external vantage point from which to gaze at the entire stretch of Western Tradition of Thinking and interrogate it from outside, as it were. For that purpose, Heidegger engaged in a conversation with Japanese Zen Monk. I believe that confrontation did not prove to be all that productive, mainly because he couldn't have known at the time that Japanese version of Zen, brought to West by

---

[26] Quoted in Zimmermann's Heidegger's Confrontation with Modernity,

Japanese scholars of Western Literature, would not have been genuinely authentic East Asian thinking.[27]

What Heidegger might have been seeking –a path to a different kind of thinking--might have been, very possibly, found by a French Philosopher and Sinologist, François Jullien. If Heideggerian historical deconstruction (strictly from within) has been found wanting, then perhaps a comparative studies with comparative criteria found from outside the Western tradition of thinking might provide unexpected clues or insights for re-configuring Modern Civilization as we know it today without ditching it altogether. Consider this tantalizingly interesting programmatic agenda for the birth of an entirely new humanistic discipline in order truly to find a way out of the current nihilist morass:

> "Because Chinese civilization, which is one of the oldest (and was recorded in texts very early on), developed without any borrowings or influences from the European West for a long time, China presents a case study through which to contemplate Western thought from the outside – and, in this way, to bring us out of our atavism.

> "Thus it is necessary to take a step back. A theoretical distancing is desirable – and this is exactly what China offers."[28]

"To contemplate Western thought from the outside" is the first step towards a REAL encounter with the historical situation in which Modern (therefore Western) Civilization is mired, and *fortiori* the real state of 'Contemporary Art' as well. Just notice, such brilliant intellects as Danto or Cavell have not been able to recognize the dire situation of "post-historical arts" as the blackest kind of 'passive' nihilism; passive Nihilists celebrate the state of 'anything goes' as plentitude of sheer 'plurality' as if it is a positive merit in itself. The active (or 'perfect' as Nietzsche sometimes also called by this name) nihilists at least exert strenuous efforts to investigate –to think through—the dire situation to the bottom of it, even if it might eventuate in his or her coming face to face with a reality one might not be able to accept –a reality so devastating as to encounter the horror of self-nullity. The modernist painters asked questions about the very nature of their craft of painting in an act of historical deconstruction of their inherited tradition with rigor and passion, even if it meant finally bringing that tradition to its end –the end of (their kind of Western)Art. Danto notwithstanding, the rigorous follow-through of the modernist deconstructive painting took them to the empty canvases of monochrome as in Ryman's or in Jules Olitski's color-field, or merely shaped literal canvas as in Frank Stella's. For Danto, that ending is the discovery of the real in place of 'art', forecasting a new beginning of 'art' now differently understood; again, it is something to be celebrated. Is this not exactly the typical Liberal Late-Capitalist attitude of voraciously co-opting any and everything in a hypocritical gesture of seeming generosity and accommodation with money, giving any and everything a token membership in society and culture –the joys of multiculturalism and pluralism, indeed; the passive nihilists are in fact 'aspect-blind' in exactly the way Wittgenstein meant. They're thus never able to get out their own atavism.

No other Western scholar before François Jullien has been able to come up with a suggestion for a way out of their (Western) atavism: it is a comparative studies of Chinese thinking vis-à-vis Western thinking. Jullien's suggestion is also applicable to the examination of the historical destinies

---

[27] See Kai Hong's contribution in 2011 Daigu City Museum Catalog as well as *Japan: A Reinterpretation* by Patrick Smith (1998) for updates on recent historical scholarships on modern Japan if there is one. One of the main theses in his book is that the Japanese failed to construct their own Modern-Japanese Identity.

[28] Francois Jullien,*Detour and Access : Strategies for Meaning in China and Greece*: p..9.

of Western Art as well. In fact, in the second Part of this Essay, I wish to suggest and make a persuasive case for a species of 'contemporary art' (but not in the sense of 'contemporary' in the way Danto, Hal Foster and their Colleagues of International Centers of Art and Culture in the hegemonic West) from South Korea that they demonstrate the possibility of genuine ART, not besmirched by Western version of 'Contemporary Art' of blackest nihilism, trapped in a vicious circle of endless endgame –mired in the midst of an abysmal black hole of nihilism[29].

PART II   Daamhua from South Korea

Is there Korean Modernist or Postmodern Art? Or, Can there be such things at all?

I voiced a lot of disagreements with Arthur Danto's accounts concerning modernism and postmodernism (or post-historicalism or the 'end-of-the- art-ism' à la Danto) in Western Art of the past century and half or so. However, I want to begin the second part of this essay, by quoting approvingly what he said about Monochrome Painting –that the very term 'monochrome painting' makes its appearance in the historical narrative of Western Art History only because the history of Western Art was ending with the internal exhaustion of the modernist narrative à la Greenberg[30]. In other words, outside the context of the Western Modernist discourse, the idea of 'monochrome painting' is conceptually empty –useless. As I've already indicated at the very outset in my introductory preamble, it is really much ado about nothing to even debate whether there's a meaningful art called 'Korean Monochrome Painting' with its own distinct matrix (or 'complex' in Danto's version) of art-practices with its own master narrative.

I suggest that what have been proposed as its master narratives are as one wanting, mere ad hoc theorizing (or philosophizing?) of neither explanatory merit nor conceptual coherence. For example, both Park Seobo and Lee Ufan insist that Korean Monochrome Painting is distinct from Western Monochrome Painting within a very singular historical dialectic of Modernist Endgame. Well, then, as Danto had an occasion to say, lying outside the modernist discursive practice of Western Painting, it is simply not helpful whether to call it 'Korean Monochrome Painting' or "Korean Dansaekua" or "Korean Tansaekhua" in explaining how and in what sense Korean Monochrome Painting is distinctly Korean or East-Asian, while most of them bear remarkable, if superficial, resemblances to Western Monochrome Paintings of Modernism[31]. I wish to suggest that it is just to do disservice to Korean Painters who had been brought to 2013 KNMMA to call them "Korean dansaekhua" without offering any clear set of guidelines for their selection. Furthermore, to be truthful, no such guideline would be available in the absence of a persuasive explanatory description of the paradigm of Korean monochrome painting. (It just won't do to vaguely mumble about their East Asian sensibility and Western techniques and matière in happy 'fusion', enabling them to come up with a distinct style of painting.) How did this unfortunate eventuality come about? Painful as it might be, it is necessary to critically-- and with no sentimentality-- interrogate Korean Art-discursive practices of the past half a century or so, whether it's done in the name of 'Western Painting' or 'Oriental Painting'.

Unfortunately, Korea was first introduced to Western Modernity through Japanese lenses, Korea having become forcibly 'annexed' (a euphemism for colonized) to Japan at the very beginning of the 20th Century. Japanese strategy for modernization was via Westernization, transplanting a complete Western nation and society, lock, stock and barrel, onto Japan. Not only political structures, juridical institutional model, but also even in art education, the Japanese wanted exactly to copy the Western Practices. In the realm of Art, therefore they began training Japanese in the ways of Western Painting,

---

[29]   Clement Greenberg, "Modernist Painting" in *Art and Culture*

[30]   Danto, *After the End of Art*, the chapter on Monochrome Painting, in passim.

[31]   Yoon Jin-seop, Catalogue Essay on Korean Dansaekhua for 2012 KNMMA exhibition.

in style, material, aesthetics, and all that. Then, as an afterthought, Japanese Government did create another, very separate discipline of 'Oriental Painting'. From then on, a Painter in Japan had to be either Western Painter or an Oriental Painter; thus, there were two distinct paradigms of painting in Japan[32]. (Koreans in their turn took over the Japanese way of dividing into two different kinds of art practices with their paradigmatic rules of the game.)

Japanese and Korean Artists of Western Painting, with rare exceptions, were not well aware of the implicitly underlying historical dialectic in the stylistic evolution of the modernist painting in the Western centers of Art. But, that was only to be expected, as they came to Western Painting from the outside, whereas all the historical dilemmas and artistic problematic of the Western Painting were the inevitable outcomes of their own peculiar historical experiences (of the West). They were, in other words, non-native speakers in the realm of Western Modernist Painting, if you will. It is for this reason that the great American formalist art critic, Clement Greenberg said of Japanese Abstract-expressionist painters: "***They came very close, but not quite. . .***"[33] Indeed, the majority of the Japanese and Korean artists of 'Western Painting' were mere imitators; they were busy-bodies, trying to catch up with all different newly emerging styles of painting and other art-practices from the International Art Centers of Paris and New York. It was not unusual to see an exhibition catalogue of Korean painters in which they paraded their exhibitions being the first such an art exhibition in Korea to import the most recently fashionable style of Paris or from New York. They were proudly stating they were the first Korean painter to do what just only recently emerged in Paris. That used to be their claim to fame and success. It was not unusual in the 70s and 80s to go to Korean art exhibitions and then come away with this feeling that I had seen all these before somewhere else; but, not all of them, by any means. Jewels can be found in a dump of ashes or among the thrown out debris. Yes, indeed, Greenberg was most definitely right when he said, "Some of them came very close, but not quite. . ." Ah, but, finally, I realized that even Clement Greenberg could have failed to notice some really surprising genuine pieces of art-historical importance to be found among Korean painters(and I'm sure also of Japanese modern painters of Western Painting).

While saying that it is vacuous to call some works of art as Korean Monochrome Painting outside the context of Western Modernist Discourse of Painting a la Greenberg; there was a minority group of painters among nearly hundred Korean painters represented at the massive 2013 KNMMA 'Dansaekhua Exhibition' whose works promise to open up an entirely new perspective on Art, never seen anywhere else until now. I propose to name them Daamhua Painters rather than Dansaekhua Painters and sketch what kind of an entirely new Art World or Horizon of Art these Daamhua Painters have already opened up, with their Daamhua Paintings. (The moniker of 'dansaekhua' is, I claim, detrimental to properly understanding the distinct kind of art, intrinsically different from what is globally understood in today's International Art Centers of the West –their style and philosophy of ***arting*** is entirely alien from the Western Modernist or Post-Historical Artists.)

The preponderant majority of Korean Modern Painters cum Dansaekhua Painters represented at the same exhibition must be classed as Monochrome Painters of Western variety of 'Modernism', practicing their art from within the bounds of the Paradigmatic Rules of Western Modernism. They're simply Korean Artists practicing Western Art, no more, no less. I believe both Park Seobo and Lee Ufan, usually considered to be the pioneering leaders and theoreticians of Korean School of Monochrome Painting belong to this group of Korean Westernized modern artists, their protestations

---

[32] Chisholm, Lawrence W., Fenollosa: the Far-East and American Culture, New Haven, Yale University Press, 1963
[33] From a personal conversation with Greenberg at his Upper West Side apartment in 1979

notwithstanding[34]. I'll shortly be discussing how and why that is so—namely, how and why their works are merely monochromatic, failing to achieve the quality of 'dam(淡). But that doesn't mean that they are not exceptionally gifted and successful artists, their works assessed from within the art-critical discursive practices of the Western Centers in much the same way Nam Jun Paik was very successful in that particular Arting game of the Western Avant-garde of whatever variety, whether in alte- or neo- mode. As for the vague references they make to some particular aspects of traditional Korean cultural resources in their works, making them distinct, albeit their Arting being squarely within the bounds of Western Game rules; they can be safely discarded. Often, such an effort to add some Korean or Oriental color or element to their otherwise completely Western Arting is just an insincere appendage as an after-thought, often merely catering to Western Orientalism, producing their works for Western viewers and Western critics. Colonial mentality is a chronic disease, difficult to get rid of in a world system where there's a center or core and a periphery and also hinterlands. (Why do so much fashionable post-colonial discourses seem so intellectually dishonest and hypocritical and opportunistic? As well for the multiculturalism!)

A Brief Digress on
Contemporary Global Art of Postmodernism/Postcolonialism/Multiculturalism:

A strange thing began to happen since roughly about two decades ago in Art-Cultural Power Centers of the rapidly globalizing World. Surreptitiously at first perhaps but in what is for all practical purposes flooding soon afterwards, 3rd World artists from the periphery and other outlying hinterlands began to be represented in the exhibition halls of up-scale galleries and museums of modern and contemporary arts in the International Cultural-Power Centers of the 1st World (mainly of the West) such as New York and London. From South Korea to Shanghai, Singapore and Spain, from London to Mumbai, Hong Kong, Tokyo and Los Angeles, virtually everywhere, all kinds of international conferences on multiculturalism, post-colonialism, international biennials, exhibitions, lectures, art fairs, have been organized; all of them eager to bring the most exotic, previously discovered, esoteric, foreign, ethnic, primitive, different artists and their supposed works of art. Many of them were once upon a time shunned by the Western centers of modern civilization but now they were eagerly embraced by Art-Cultural institutions of the West. What is all this about? This *internationalization* (or should it be *globalization*, rather?) of any and all species of 'multicultural arts'? This inclusion of cultural diversity, this acceptance and commodification of all kinds of art from the peripheries, into the main-stream global contemporary culture: what does it all mean? These are urgent and important questions to ask, albeit that there're usual pat answers and ready explanations in the positive by the proponents of the post-colonial discourse such as its luminary Homi Bhabha of Harvard University[35].

---

[34] Park Seobo painstakingly composes beforehand and has his assistants finish or realize. That is purely Western Style; it goes against the Genuine Spirit of Art of Ancient East Asia. So is the case with Lee Ufan; in spite of his postures as Japanese Zen Practitioner, his art-practice is directly opposed to what is authentically Zen experience. He, for example, paints and represents the Brushstrokes, instead of actually move his body for that brushstroke. There's no brushstroke but only painted false brushstrokes. His is not the Art of brush-strokes but of painted brush-strokes. You don't pre-plan, think and compose in Oriental Zen Painting; you just let go of your body and hands, not guided by your intellect or willful will to do this way or that way. For those not familiar with this way of Arting, it might be helpful to refer to Francois Jullien's elegantly contrasting of the East-Asian and Western ways of Arting. See for example, Jullien,

[35] Homi Bhabha,"Cultural Diversity and Cultural Differences" [from ATLAS OF TRANSFORMATION] or his Location of Culture,

At any scene of International Contemporary Art, whether it is an International Art Fair or an International Biennial, one is most likely to see a rag-tag multicultural collection of arts from everywhere, taking a special care that some from really remote periphery countries are included. (For example, Kassel Dokumenta went quite out of the way to get INUIT artists from the truly remote area of the Arctic.) Then, too, as a rule so to speak, there'd be a handsome volume of an exhibition catalogue, with a long-winded variations on the similar theme of some ready-made cultural theoretical formulae of post-colonial, multicultural or post-modern discourses. We could surmise from all these facts that the true definition of "International Contemporary Art" at all those International Biennials is the entire set of all the art-products done by all the working artists from all corners of the world of all different cultural traditions, contemporaneous to one another from, with the word "contemporaneous" understood from the historic-temporal point of view of 'now'.

Many of these artists from the third world countries on the periphery have, often, become globe-trotters, moving from International Biennial to another, representing their respective cultural particularities; increasingly, they'd adopt the so-called "post-modern" idioms of Western Art-Practices, as the Chinese have done to create their own style of C-Pop. They appropriated New York version of Pop-Art as stylistic devices for 'historically deconstructing' their recent history under Maoism, giving gleeful expression to their newly discovered artistic freedom. (Only a single style of Social Realism was allowed them under Chinese Communism until Deng Shao-Ping came up with Chinese version of "Cultural Thaw".[36]) So, you see the same mutually cloning or cloned works of Installation Arts, conceptually inspired or based on some variation of some traditional cultural theme from the Artists' own cultural traditions; also ubiquitous are some art things that are supposed to have been Video or Technologically mediated or composed, again their artistic motifs gleaned from diverse allegedly traditional cultural particularities of their own. What should be noticed is that no matter where on earth their works are shown, whether Kwangju Biennial or at Mumbai or Shenzen or Timbuktu, the artists are actually all interested in entering into good business relationships with the International Main-Stream Cultural Powers That Be well-ensconced at International Cultural Centers of Western Metropolises such as New York, London, Berlin and Paris. It is basically the same logic under which the Colonial subjects had to learn, however awkwardly, their Colonial Masters' Language in order to make themselves understood to the Masters on the occasions of cultural, political and economic negotiations.

According to Post-Colonial theories a la Bhabha, for instance, the Colonial subject's transaction with his Master from the West is not for that reason just one-sided power-relation of the dominant over the dominated. On the contrary, in that space of time-lag bound to occur, for the Colonial's inadequate mastering of his Master's language would create moments of hesitation in the very act of cultural negotiation, coming from two different cultures. The Colonial's inarticulateness, cultural differences and traces of tradition-bound thinking --albeit his Western ways of education—would create an interstice of indeterminacy of cultural interpretations, slyly creating an opportunity of undermining the Colonial Master's certainty of his being in control by casting doubt on the Master's

---

[36] A term used to refer to Khrushchev's de-Stalinization policies begun in 1953. See, for example,
William Taubman's Khrushchev: the Man and his Era, London, Free Press, 2004.

ability to rationally understand the situation, thereby finding a way to subversively turn the negation in his favor for some tiny profit. He had to mimic, imitate, if inadequately his Master's language and cultural mores in order to make himself understood and into his confidence. In such cultural dynamics, a Colonial becomes inadvertently a betrayer of his own cultural tradition in adopting Western ways, while not being accepted into his Master's Class, remaining a permanent Other as a Colonial forever. Yet, this cultural Hybrid is, perhaps without knowing it himself, is a cultural Subversive, slyly in many subterfuge ways, undermining the superiority of the Colonial Master. With massive immigration from the former Colonies to the Colonized countries after World War II of the Post-Colonial Period, the former Colonials have become not insignificant minority population blocks of the so-called Hegemonic Center countries of the First World of the West: their sheer presence in the midst of the Western 'Lebenswelt' (a la Husserl) subtly transforming it on the way to creating a "Subaltern Cosmopolitan Culture on a global scale."[37]

Likewise, then, the International Contemporary Art of multiculturalism today is the testimony to the success of Globalization via Hybridization? Perhaps, this outcome might be a cause for a gleeful celebration on the part of the Neo-Liberals who's been pushing for Economic/Financial/Trade globalization for the past three or four decades, trying to harness all nations on the Planet Earth under the same System of economic-financial regulations, imposing the same kind of Business Culture, so to speak. What the theorists of the Post-colonialist discourse such as Homi Bhabha have called the subversive undermining of the dominant class by the dominated through cultural-hybridization mounts only to a Pyrrhic victory, if at all. Furthermore, these Multiculturalists cum Post-colonialists cum Postmodernists have utterly misread the Current Crisis of the Mankind from an Epochal[38] perspective (a la Heidegger, for example); they have inadvertently lent a ruse for the ***Global Powers That Be*** to continue to dominate under the false pretense of liberal acceptances of the sheer diversity, pluralism and multiculturalism. One wonders if Bhabha and his colleagues are not secret agents for the Dominant whose role is to defuse-- through cleverly disguised means of co-optation-- any sort of efforts to change the global power relationship in all sectors of economy, politics, culture, art and sciences. At most, through hybridization, only a few Colonials have joined the Main-stream Western establishment; is it not true that under political slogans of multiculturalism, post-colonialism and such likes, a coterie of subalterns have joined the Western main-stream academic, artistic and cultural establishments, while disarming any serious intellectual, political and moral efforts on the part of the "wretched of the earth" to find their true voice and bona-fide equal

---

[37] Postcolonial theorists have misappropriated this term from Italian Marxist, Antonio Gramsci for their allegedly "revolutionary" purposes. See, for example, Homi Bhabha, "Unsatisfied: notes on vernacular cosmopolitanism." *Text and Nation: Cross-Disciplinary Essays on Cultural and National Identities*, Edited by Laura Garcia-Moreno and Peter C. Pfeiffer. Columbia, SC: Camden House, 1996: 191-207.

[38] Postcolonial theorists are like one, whether it's Bhabha or Spivak, Derridarean Deconstructionists. Their problem is that Derridarean Deconstruction is proving out to be misappropriation of Heidegger's "Destruzione," having failed to see that Heidegger's later writings provide very important insights into the notion of "Destruzione" as something much more complex and profound than Derridareans had previously thought, requiring a proper appreciation of Epochal Principles. Reiner Schürmann has brilliantly and single-handedly what had never been done before in Heidegger scholarship by articulating the architectonics of Heideggerian philosophical project lying across and over the huge body of his philosophical writings. It was nothing less than a heroic intellectual effort on his part and the result is his acclaimed last book, *Heidegger on Acting and Anarchy: From Principles to Anarchy*.

humanity of their manhood by overturning the seemingly permanent power-relationships of the modern world. (Is it any wonder then that Bhabha has been accused of emasculating Fanon of his true liberationist/revolutionary politics?)

Globalization and Global (International) Culture: a historical destiny? We can agree with the theorists of "post-colonialism" that there's indeed been a cultural-globalization going on for quite a long time already at least since the time of Industrial Revolution, initiated by the invention of the first "steam engine" in 1784 in England. However, the intellectual ground for such a technological break-through had been laid down in the emergence of a New World View, first given articulation in Issac Newton's new Physics and Rene Descartes' "new method" of (analytical) thinking –later to be known as "Newtonian-Cartesian" paradigm [cum] world-view. Modern Age thus began with an entirely new ways of looking at and thinking about the world; and the technological-industrial revolution was the initiation of an entirely new ways of living—the transformation of concrete living realities. In short, Newton-Cartesian articulation of a rational/methodical ways of thinking and understanding universe and matter of the things in nature and from within that paradigm of thinking, industrial technological innovations and inventions began to occur –the invention of steam engine and then the electric motor among others. Once on, one scientific breakthrough followed upon on another and another and so on; likewise with technological inventions, one after another and on. Engines powered by steam and later by electricity drove Rail Road Trains and Ocean-going Ships throughout the world over land and sea. They also powered factory machines of mass production, recruiting industrial workers in massive numbers, making the countryside near empty. Massive industrial employment, uprooted from lands, as wage workers at factories and coal mines, required an entirely new ways of social organization, as fast urbanization with the continuously arriving new factory workers occurred where there were many factories of mass production came together for mutual convenience in industrial networking of a sort, already making appearance on the national industrialized-economic affairs. Industrial development had its own developmental logic and systems requirements as preconditions for further developments. Systems requirement for industrial development was actually nothing other than Network Logic, for different industries need to network with one another in parallel or hierarchical ways of logic. Since mass production factory machineries required the supplies of electric power, power plants had to be built at strategic geographic locations, a network of power transmission lines had to be created all over the nation, but the building of power plants had to be planned, financed and managed in an efficient nation-wide system. Raw material had to be mined or imported through international trades and then transported to the factory. The huge number of industrial workers had to be housed, their children fed and educated, their health services taken care of. In short, industrial development required industrial workers trained in new disciplinary ways, with new ways of thinking and acting on factory floors. Their managers needed to think in a more systematic rational ways than the former farm managers. Industrial developments are powered by newer and newer technological inventions. Industrial civilization powered and configured by the logic and requirements of technology as an overarching, all-inclusive system of thinking and organization is nothing other than an ideology or a religion as famously put by Martin

Heidegger, the one person who had most profoundly meditated on the nature of modern technology as an over-arching and overpowering complex system.[39]

Modern technology, given birth by the new ways of thinking about nature's way (or its mechanics) initiated by Isaac Newton--as an all-inclusive complex system-- required its own *systems-thinking* and socio-political-economic organization of the society or the nation state. Modern Technological thinking is culture- and ethnic- independent; its logic is universalistic. It is for this reason that the great French Philosopher, Paul Ricoeur despaired at the seemingly necessary, inevitable accompaniment of any industrial development in any nation state ending up with a cultural transformation at the same into a ways of life pretty much similar to that emerged in America, the first Mass Consumer Society of a technological society[40]. This can be seen in South Korea today, for example, in the very American ways of life average Koreans are living, their mobility entirely automobile based, their shopping style at shopping mauls, their children's education curricula and school culture as well as college campus culture, in the way South Koreans today eat, drink and dress, they are just like Americans other than their yellow faces. The cityscapes in urban centers such as Seoul and Busan are clones of American metropolises with the same ubiquitous high-rise concrete and glass towers. Tokyo, Hong Kong and Shanghai, they are no different from Seoul and also from London or New York in sheer appearance and in the way they are managed (or is it administered).

In short, the cultural globalization is more of a necessary but subsidiary by-product of industrialization (with its own internal requirements as necessary preconditions such as the necessary socio-political modernization via rationalization of the national life of the state) than it's an achievement through any sort of intercultural negotiation in its interstice as Bhabha et al would make us believe. Modern technology is a voracious power-mongering, with its own international systems logic, ultimately dictating the very humanity into its submission, with the potential of even changing the very human nature when its technological systems logic is taken to its luminal point). It is this Productionist Metaphysics of the West that's been creating a set of entirely new ontological existents called "Hyper Objects"[41], mounting danger to all life forms and to the very ecological system the healthy maintenance of which is the very condition for the life forms of all different kinds for their survival and flourish. The theorists of Post-colonialism have nothing to say about this historical situation, mired in the endless end-game playing of nihilism. The same goes for the artists of the International Contemporary Art. Instead of perceiving with historical acuity the Epochal demands and addressing them as creative artists, they are all in collusion –if inadvertently-- with the Neo-liberal Greed Capitalists who care only for their own kind's continuous power of global domination in false guises of genial acceptance of diversities by playing tokens of diversity without genuine cross-cultural dialogues, while betraying their brethren back in their native lands mired in the same position of the dominated, with lives no better for their token representation in the mainstream

---

[39] Heidegger, *Questions Concerning Technology*

[40] Paul Ricoeur, "Universal Civilization and National Culture" (1961), *History and Truth*, trans. Charles A. Kelbley. Evanston: Northwestern University press. 1965, pp.276-7.

[41] Timothy Morton, *Hyper objects: Philosophy and Ecology after the End of the World*, University of Minnesota Press, 2013

centers. Heidegger looked to Art, in its genuine sense of the very term, as a possible antidote to Technological Nihilism pervasive in all the so-called already modernized parts of the World (via industrialization according to the systems logic of technology, the modern religion).

"Our age demands art that is intrinsically different from what is widely accepted as art."[42] ***Damhua from South Korea answers the call?***

> "Alright, the Art is Dead now; but the question still remains – as question – of the possibility of a great art (that is, an art comparable to Greek Art), and it remains all the more as a question in that the beginnings of a response can only be found if –and only if – thought will be capable of speaking of art in another language than that of aesthetics which is the language of the whole of philosophy since Plato and Aristotle, i.e., precisely since the end of great Art."[43]
>
> --Lacoue-Labarthe

After the end of art came with the internal exhaustion of the modernism of Western Art, a state of anomie reigns and the situation of 'anything' goes prevails over the entire landscape of Western Art World. Douglas Crimp seemed to have mourned the situation of "pervasive possibility of fraudulence" –i.e., anything goes; while in the meantime Hal Foster became one of the most prominent advocates of the postmodernism and later neo-avant-garde and other such apologist theories for some of those "anything-goes!" variety of all kinds of non-senses masquerading as the most theoretically-sophisticated and advanced experimental artists. Belatedly, however, Hal Foster seems to admit that he'd erred in taking the once fashionable postmodernist and neo-avant-garde discourses that he once advocated have all run into sand, at least in his recent "Dan Flavin and the Catastrophe of Minimalism."

I find it odd that Danto and Hal Foster, supposedly two of the most brilliant theorists of modern and postmodern (or post-historical) art, failed to see that any kinds of explanatory discursive practices -- whether in the name of postmodernism, neo-avant-garde, minimal, art-povera, earthwork, or whatever else – can only be ***post hoc, ad hoc***, artificial patched-up theories and no more. Danto says himself that any art after the end of art cannot stand by itself as an example of art (after the end of art). As such, indeed, post-historical artists always seem to have the need to offer some sort of justificatory ad hoc theories, whenever they do a gallery or museum show, as in the case of Joseph Kosuth, for example. I find it utterly preposterous that a respected Analytic Philosopher of Danto's reputation cites this self-proclaimed conceptual artist, approvingly, as the very model of a new breed of "post-historical artists whose very art-practices are in fact nothing other than to philosophize about art." One of the results of this Dantoesque post-historical Artist's philosophizing about Art is a short text in English, titled "Art as Philosophy." I, for one, had never read anything more idiotic than the gibberish text. As a piece of writing, not to speak of it being a philosophical writing, it is simply gibberish nonsense. Are we, then, given to think that viewed as an instance of a post-historical conceptual art, this sheer idiocy is alchemically turned into a brilliant creative act? While the works he produces may be exemplary instances of the "post-historical Art" a la Danto; Kosuth's kinds of post-historical art fits more perfectly into the mold that will never rise above the condition of the "pervasive possibility of fraudulence" as characterized by Cavell.

People like him and the likes of Damien Hearst can strut around as a Post-Historical Star Artist, garnering awards and fellowships from Federal and/or State Government Agencies. In a

---

[42] Lacoue-Labarthe, ***Heidegger, Art and Politics***, p.57
[43] Ibid.

historical condition in which there's no (implicitly) accepted set of criteria by which to judge if something is Art or Not, it is just a question of who's a better snake-oil seller or a junk-bond dealer. That's why no one has the gall to call such false prophets as the many varieties of Conceptual Artists are in the Art World to their face that "Yours have '***Nothing Whatsoever To Do With Art***'." The modernist predicament in the Contemporary Westernized Global Art is this: Nothing can be discounted as Art, but by the same token nothing can be legitimized as Art either. In that nether world of Neither Art nor Not-Art, all kinds of idiots are posturing, self-marketing themselves as great artists, easily spotted at so many International Art Biennales whether it's Cassel Dokumenta, Venice, Kwangju, Sao Paulo, Beijing, Timbuktu or wherever else as the *'influenza area'* –in the sense of the term Wittgenstein used--from which to infect the rest of the world with the lethal virus of blackest kind of nihilism of our Age.

It should also be pointed out that there's a reason—albeit mistakenly, as I shall show -- for Danto's characterization of post-historical art as not being able to stand on its own but requiring some sort of, however stupid, ad hoc theories or complex of theories to explain[it].[44] In a nutshell, Danto sees an enlightening comparison possible between a primitive tribe which had no prior contact with the outside world before and post-historical neo-avant-garde tribe of artists. To a cultural anthropologist who just chanced upon some primitive tribe, no linguistic (verbal) communication is possible for now; before deciphering the grammar and vocabulary of their tribal language, each and every verbal utterance from them would merely be just any gibberish or just something utterly incomprehensible. But of course the tribal utterances are not just any gibberish; it's just that the cultural anthropologist hasn't learned their language. Danto is saying, likewise with the tribe of post-historical avant-garde artists whose artistic-gestures are in fact just any gibberish of "anything goes" variety. But just as our cultural anthropologist will begin with patient observation of the primitive's verbal behavior, theorizing about the relationships between their bodily gestures and their verbal utterances in his or her painstaking process of (scientific-) discovery of their grammar; post-historical art critics and theorists have to play the role of the cultural anthropologist vis-à-vis post-historical avant-garde artists' "any gibberish" *(f-) Arting* as a new species of (post-historical) Art. Just like our intelligent cultural anthropologist, Danto, Hal Foster, or any other theorists of post-historical Art have no choice but to engage in making up some sort of theories about post-historical ways of *Arting* as heuristic devices for continuing (scientific/cum theoretical) investigation.

I believe Danto's totally mistaken and misguided in his application of Quine's story of a cultural anthropologist's discovering of a primitive tribal language through theory-construction to the understanding of post-historical avant-garde artists' *Arting* behaviors. The primitives have always had a language already and therefore their grammar was there to be discovered, whereas the avant-garde artists have not had any language until they came up with an ad hoc artifice as a post hoc justification of their pointless and meaningless gestures, the point and meaning of which they themselves are not even clear about. It is incredible that this flimsy and false comparison has not been exposed and that Danto's flimsy account of Avant-garde Arting behavior had gained respecible reception among the discourse-generators of the Contemporary Westernized Global Art World. No amount of such a flimsy apologist theoretical efforts can delay the inevitable expose of the Nihilist Face of Western Avant-garde (or Modernism or Post-Modernism) that have been masquerading as 'advanced art' –yes, this beloved term which seem to recur in Danto's and Hal Foster's essay, articles and books.

---

[44] The "it "here is the post-historical art being presented in whatever shape and form such as 'installation', light show, video performance or some spectacle like Christo's.

The point I'm trying to get across is so important that I wish to recount it one more time at the risk of repetitiousness. The situation of post-historical art is so singular in its entire stretch of Western History that any art critic or theorists of post-historical art must assume the attitude of a cultural anthropologist who has just come across a primitive tribe. Post-historical avant-garde artists are the Post-historical art critics' primitives. Only from what they [the post-historical artists] actually do in the name of art, can you derive an understanding of post-historical art and whatever rules of the game of *arting* they're engaged in. Minimalism, Postmodernism, Neo-avant-garde and whatever else are all competing theories of the post-historical avant-garde artists' behavior of *arting*. Danto's analogy doesn't of course hold as we indicated in the previous paragraph. Danto's celebration of the sheer plurality of "anything goes" notwithstanding; an equally persuasive and superior standpoint is there to take: it is to look upon the untenable situation of post-historical art as that of nihilist end-game with no possibility of an exit. In other words, the post-historical artists (or the artists after the end of art) are just nihilist frauds, pretenders, hardly deserving the moniker of the "practitioners of the most *advanced* art in today's world. (I notice that both Danto and Hal Foster seem to use this term quite often, confident that they're situated at the very hegemonic center of the world today and fortiori whatever being done in their town in whatever realm must be the most advance, be it in the Arts, Music, Sciences, fashion or whatever else.)

In such a dire historical situation of post-historical art trapped in the midst of blackest nihilism, no new direction of art or no new beginning can be conceivable, not to speak of finding or deriving from within the internally exhausted intellectual, spiritual and cultural resources of the Western Civilization. French Philosopher, Lacoue-Labarthe echoes Martin Heidegger's foresights over the historical destiny of Western Art, *"Our age demands art that is intrinsically different from what is widely accepted as art."* What can this art be? Certainly not Danto's version of post-historical art; for it is just a euphemism for nihilism, the very sounding of this word, an ideological leading light of Americanism (of technopian nature) of his caliber cannot voice even in silence, perhaps. Instead of the vacuous discourses of Contemporary Art as post-historical or post-modern Art, we'd want a new art that is foundational in an altogether different sense of the term. Otherwise, we will continue to be mired in nihilist end-game-playing with nil prospect for the humanity, unless one is willing to embrace another nightmarish future in which men are transformed into mechanical beings on the par with any other kinds of mass-produced industrial products, perhaps higher-IQ'ed Cyborgs or AI-ed AH (Artificial Humanoids), as the Priests of the technopian religion of Americanism, the Futurologists Professors and Consultants, the Technopolyanas will do perfectly.

In other words, the Art that our Age demands, therefore, is a "Great Art, an art that is - comparable to Greek Art but is capable of being thought of in "another language than that of aesthetics which is the language of the whole of philosophy since Plato and Aristotle."[45] The Art that our Age demands cannot be what today goes under the name 'of "Contemporary Art" in Danto's philosophico-theoretical articulation, in spite of his version of post-historical art falling outside the conceptual purview of Aesthetics. There actually is an art that is "intrinsically different from what is widely accepted as art and is capable of being thought of in a language other than that of aesthetics (as this term is conceptualized in Western tradition of philosophy): it is Art as it was once practiced in Ancient East Asia. As Francois Jullien so brilliantly delineated the radical difference of East Asian Art (it is 'Chinese Art' for Jullien in his rough grouping of all that is Northeast Asia of millennia or two ago) from Western conception of Art until its demise as in The End of Art a la Danto, Crimp, Hal Foster, Belting et al. In Ancient Northeast Asian world of art, in their way of thinking of art; they had no need for such a discipline and notion of 'aesthetics'. (In a slim volume of NUDE: Chinese Art and Western Aesthetics, Francois Jullien does a marvelous job of contrasting two entirely incommensurable conceptual-philosophical systems of thinking and yet each capable of

---

[45] Lacoue-Labarthe, Heidegger, <u>Art and Politics,</u>

creating equally great culture and civilization (and of course also of great specimen of artistic achievements).[46]

I suggest that the New Great Art (in the sense of Greek Art) capable of becoming foundational is emerging and that what I call 'daamhua' Painting from South Korea is the harbinger, if not yet full-fledged, of the next 'Great Art', capable **re-configuring** globally Westernized (or 'Americanized' in the sense of Paul Ricoeur) Culture and therefore Contemporary Art (as a global phenomenon) as well. Let me explain:

So, What Then IS Daamhua(淡畫)?

What species of Art does it [this *daamhua*] promise to show the world? One might very likely challenge me at this point: "Well, after all, they were already presented at last year's KNMMA 'dansaekhua' exhibition for everyone to see. It is in the past tense already. So, how can you talk about what they promise to show in the future tense?" It's just that everyone failed to see what promise they held within them, seeing them through Western or Westernized filters of Modernism or Postmodernism or some other such unhelpful and misguided intellectual frameworks. My first thesis is this: daamhua painting exemplify the "art that is intrinsically different from what is widely accepted as art" in today's globalized art world and cultural context. Then, one of the first corollaries derivable from this thesis would be that there is an alternative conceptual system of discursive practices concerning art, definable in a language other than that of Western Aesthetics, and that it is readily describable. In what follows, I intend to borrow heavily from Jullien's brilliant presentation of Eastasian Philosophy of Art in which they have no need for the Western philosophical sub-discipline of Aesthetics, especially from his masterpiece, The Impossibility of Nude: Chinese Art and Western Aesthetics.[47]

Lee U-fan has been the most important practitioner and early theoretician of Korean Monochrome Painting. This unabashed Japanophile Korean-born Japanese Artist and Critic derives, in his artistic and critical cum theoretical practices, nearly all of his ideas and also discursive terms from Nishida Kitaro and his students' formulation of Zen-experience. In other words, Lee has been claiming that Japanese and Korean Monochrome Painting is nothing other than modernist version of Zen-Art, later, of course, it would become Post-Modern version of Zen-Art, while nothing has been changed in his actual *Arting* practices. **(That Lee Ufan can call his version of Zen Art as Modern and also as Post-modern at his convenience is indicative of his theoretical/philosophical illogic or dis-rigor in his thinking. Nothing less.)** Even if we grant him his theoretical claims about Korean and Japanese Monochrome Painting, it needs to be pointed out: that in his strictly Japanese version of Zen experience and Zen Art, Nishida's notion of Absolute Nothingness is the theoretical fulcrum of Lee U-fan's narrative of modernist Zen Art (or post-modern Zenish Japanese minimalism or whatever else). But, now, what if Nishida's formulation of Zen-experience is in error? What if Nishida's is merely a half-hazardously, mechanically Westernized version of Zen, authenticity of which had been already compromised when it [Zen] was brought into Japan a millennium ago? Then, together with Nishida, notwithstanding Lee U-fan's protestations, his version of Japanized Modernist Version of Japanized Zen Art has its problems. No? This is the reason why I don't select him as one of the Daamhua Painters. As Japanized Modernist Zenish Artist of Monochrome Painting, his art has not much to offer and is open to the charges of cultural fraudulence in the sense of the term as used by Stanley Cavell in his characterization of situation of modern art as the "pervasive possibility of

---

[46] Francois Jullien, The Impossibility of Nude: Chinese Art and Western Aesthetics, Zone Book, MIT Press

[47] Francois Jullien's Zone book from MIT Press

fraudulence" and bad faith. (***Therefore, this modifier of 'fraudulent' is not being applied to the individual Lee U-fan but strictly to his Art only.***)

So, how about Nishida? The acknowledged progenitor of 'modern' Japanese Philosophy is Nishida Kitaro who attempted to formulate Zen experience in conceptual terms of Western Metaphysics. While accepting that Bergson's notion of 'intuition' seems to come very close to capturing the "pure experience" cum Zen-experience; Nishida rejects it as not philosophical. "Even if its contents are derivable from Intuition, philosophy has its reason d'être when intuition takes the form of conceptual knowledge."[48] Instead, he proposes to lay a new conceptual foundation for (Western) philosophy by re-interpreting Zen-experience in Western Metaphysical terms. For that purpose, he comes up with a variety of conceptual terms such as pure experience, pure knowledge, self-awareness and absolute nothingness. His last grand formulation for Philosophy (considering himself doing Western Philosophy in Western logical terms) is the philosophical thesis that pure experience cum Bergsonian 'intuition' is possible if and only if the subject is capable of shedding his or her subjectivity in encountering nothingness (which is possible during a Zen meditation, for example). In other words, Nishida wished him himself and us to think from the perspective of the 'place' ('topoi' or 'world' are also used, within which are the subject itself among other minds and other things in some configuration). I for one think his are desperate and clumsy efforts to translate and even brutally force East-Asian Zenish experience into the conceptual boxes of Western Metaphysics. (Is this again no different from early Japanese modernizers' wishing to become Westerners in mind, body and soul, if they could –be it Western Philosopher, Western Artist or what have you—in their efforts to shed their Asian identity of racial and cultural and spiritual kinds so rampant in Japan during Meiji Restoration periods[49]).

Nishida's entire philosophical project has been, from its very inception, misguided, for authentic articulation of what is genuine East-Asian ('philosophical') thinking and (pure) experience. He didn't take seriously the distinct possibility that Zen thinking, if there's such an animal, might be INCOMMENSURIBLE with Western thinking—that of the Metaphysical tradition of the West. Personally, when I began belatedly to study ancient East-Asian (of Korean version) spiritual practice of ***Suhaeng(修行)*** of ***Seon-ga (仙家)*** tradition; I came across a stunning lesson of awakening – that Northeast Asian Learning ('Dongyanghak'東洋學) cannot be done 100% theoretically, strictly texts-based as it can be done with Western Way of Learning ('Seoyanghak'西洋學) and that Dongyanghak must accompany hands-on ***Suhaeng***[50].

Only recently, only less than half a dozen years ago, did I come across a genuine, eye-opening lesson that this ***Suhaeng(修行) is simply the most important key word in any characterization of Northeast Asian spiritual-cultural form of life, being the fundamental basis of their way of life. And, what Nishida and others of the so-called Kyodo School of Zen Philosophy and Lee U-fan***

---

[48] 1923, "Tetsugaku" [Philosophy] in *Tetsugaku jiten* [Dictionary of Philosophy], Tokyo: Iwanami., p.668.
[49] One of the main leading lights of Japanese modernization via Westernization was the founder of Keio University who advocated the Japanese shedding of their Asian identity. Many books appeared in which they wanted prove that Japanese were actually racially not Asiatic but Caucasian in origin, tracing their distant ancestry to Ainu of Hokkaido, a distinct minority who had previously discriminated and suppressed.
[50] 朴炫, *나를 다시 하는 東洋學*,

failed to grasp is this very fact – of the singular importance of Suhaeng as simultaneously bodily and spiritual exercises, integrated into the very fabric of ordinary life of the people.

I propose henceforth to use this term, Suhaeng, as there simply is no English equivalent. This Suhaeng-based form of life of the ancient Northeast Asians is another reason for aligning with Jullien's astute understanding of the real and *genuine incommensurability between East-Asian and Western thinking* with different grammatical structures. Seon or Ch'an Meditation Practice is an important but only one element of Suhaeng-training. In *Suhaeng*, it is not the state of Absolute Nothingness one tries to arrive at; such a notion is in fact incomprehensible –nonsensical pseudo philosophizing at best. If you reach the state of absolute nothingness, it simply means you're dead, no more, even before you can have any sort of pure intuition or experience. Yes, in some state, as we will come back to, of mind and body when it is possible the "I" of your-self sort of dissolves and begins to resonate with the surrounding [call it the whole of nature or universe or some larger than you or the totality, depending on which discursive framework you work in.]. But that still has nothing to do embracing Absolute Nothingness.

Let me point out additionally, for example, that Quantum field theory helps us to reject the very idea of Absolute Nothingness à la Nishida as ill-informed, for particles are created with the help of energy present in "vacuums".   According to the most advanced theoretical physics of today -- in formulations of such leading physicists as Frank Wilczek, Stephen Hawking and some others of their Colleagues; vacuums have energy and energy is convertible into mass in that famous equation of $E = MC^2$. The conclusion is that vacuums are not empty and explains why there is something rather than nothing[51]. Just meditate on what Victor Hugo had to say on nothingness in his *Les Misérables*: "All roads are blocked to a philosophy which reduces everything to the word 'no.' To 'no' there is only one answer and that is 'yes.' Nihilism has no substance. There is no such thing as nothingness, and zero does not exist. Everything is something. Nothing is nothing! Man lives more by affirmation than by bread."[52] To always say 'No' is Nihilism. Come to think about it, there's always been an element of Nihilism in Japanese version of Samurai Zen in which the Sword and Self-Immolation have been celebrated in such words as "You live by dying, " a possibly evocative metaphor but without any explanatory force. It's a short step from there to what happened during WWII; so many young men willingly going to meet the death as Kamikaze pilot as a gesture of highest spiritual fulfillment. What if Nishida's and DK Suzuki's version of Samurai Zen had something to do with those deluded self-sacrifices in their headlong and eager embracing of the Absolute Nothingness? Does it make for a serious Metaphysics? How seriously should we take Nishida as a thinker? And now a creeping doubt

---

[51] It has to do with the symmetry of matter and anti-matter. "Given that the symmetry implies equality, matter and anti-matter should have annihilated each other. Creation should have been aborted. Why is there NOW something (particles) rather than nothing (mere energy in a quantum field)? This question was answered by calculations suggesting that there was about a billionth more matter than anti-matter. Although it is still possible for the universe to be without particles, the slight numeric imbalance biases the universe toward states in which there are many particles."

[52] Hugo, Victor, 1862, *Les Misérables.*

as to how sincere DK Suzuki was in his passionate spreading of Japanese version of Zen, Zen philosophy and Zen Art in Post WWII America?

Seon-ga(仙家) Suhaeng(修行)in state of daam-daam(淡淡)Mind(心)

The tradition Seon-Suhaen(仙修 行) is preserved only in Korea, passed down from Ancient Ancestors of Korean people(the 東夷 "Dong-yi " people), it is not to arrive at the state of Absolute Emptiness and embrace the Absolute Nothingness in order to have the *pure* kind of Zen-experience. In place of nothingness which you encounter as a result of absolute emptying of your mind as in Japanese Zen practices; it is rather to arrive at the state of *daamness* in Korean *Seon-Suhaeng*. So, let us begin with this mysterious notion of *'daam'* (淡) before anything can be said about daamhua, being presented as an entirely new species of the Art of Painting, Art understood intrinsically differently from what is understood widely –globally today.

Ah, yes, finally about this idea of *'daam (淡)'*, this Chinese character (ideogram) which Jullien translated as '*Fadeur*' in French and then in an English translator's hands as 'Blandness' in English. In spite of his Genius, I suggest that he missed an important aspect this concept and in the English translator's hands it even became semantically distorted. 'Daam' can mean, in its lexical meaning, 'bland', 'colorless', 'clear', 'serene', 'disinterested', unshakable, among others. But it is the semantic component of being calm as a result of having settled down or having been settled, captures the singularly important conceptual nucleus of this term, this word, this ideogram of 'daam'.. Its semantic twin is probably another Chinese ideogram (1)瀞 =(2)淨 + (3)靜. [淨] means 'clean' as in "to clean' or 'to purify', whereas [靜]means 'quiet', 'peace', 'inactivity', 'get quiet', 'calm'. Therefore, as a result of being stilled in inactivity, things become settled and calm and quietude prevails in 靜; being still and quiet, clarity, clearness, purity and transparency is achieved. Imagine a body of turbulent body of water. Let it sit still in inactivity, preventing nothing to enter and stir up further turbulence; in good time, the body water is stilled, calmed, all kinds of impure elements in turbulent motion settled down at the bottom. Now the body of water is not only still, calm and quiet, it is also clear, so purified and clear that one look down through the depth to the very bottom at the settled-down sediment. Notice that this is nothing other than the very *raisons d'être* for the ancient East Asian tradition of spiritual training of Taoist practices or somewhat similarly the *'Seon'(禪)* meditation.[53]

You strive, through breathing exercises, to achieve the state of daamness by stilling your breathing even and quiet –in other words let your turbulent mind settle down in inactivity—and achieve the calmed state of mind, a settled state of your body, mind and emotion; then and only then, like a clear water, would you be able to see your very own self (objectively, as it were) as well as things and phenomena of the world with clarity for what they are, unclouded by any sort of theories, prejudices, habitual ways of perception and such. This is not the same as emptying your mind in order to achieve Absolute Nothingness as the former Fascist cum Militarist Ideologue of Japan theorized Zen experience in the philosophical idioms of the Western Philosophical School of Phenomenology. (Should we be charitable towards Nishida and his students' erroneous application of the notion of Absolute Nothingness for explicating Japanese version of Zen experience? After all, just consider the kind of egregious mistakes such a great and once extremely fashionable and influential J.P. Sartre's mistaken exegesis of Heidegger in his famous book, Being and Nothingness,

---

[53] Seon or Ch'uan is better known in the West as Zen meditation. This is unfortunate, as Japanese version is an adulterated version imported into Japan from China via Chosen-Korea. Just consider the Samurai Zen of Japan which provided active ideological legitimacy to Japanese Fascism of the first half of the 20th Century.

which now is still a must-text only for the literature people, whereas the professional philosophers all agree that Sartre's is an impoverished misunderstanding of Heidegger's much more profound meditations on the destiny of Western Thought and Western Civilization.)

Allow me to digress a little, for what I propose to interject at this point is critically important in understanding the problematic of the state of academic East Asian Studies and what it might take to get away from those politically, ideologically determined dominant discursive practices on and about East Asian culture and civilization, including their arts. In other words, there's still today rampant Orientalism in Western viewing of East Asia and East Asian Culture. Still pervasive Orientalism, difficult to perceive as such, has to do with Japan. As the first Asian nation to modernize through Westernization and industrialization, Japan served as the window to the rest of East Asia. What is known as Zen Meditation of Zen Buddhism, Zen Art, etc. in the West, mainly as uniquely Japanese in origin is actually a cultural import from China and also from Korea? Furthermore, in their zeal to completely make-over all aspects of Japanese society and culture during the initial modernization process, they also repackaged their traditional cultural products to cater to Western Orientalism. There has been recent studies by social scientists and historians trying on the topic of how and why Japan whose economic and financial prowess was seemingly unchallengeable during the 1980s and into the early part of the 1990s fell so fast and so easily flat on their face, mired in perennial economic slump so much so that the corporate names of Sony or Matsushida or Toshiba, once the very symbol of Japanese Industrial Power have been far outstripped by South Korea's Samsung or LG, an event unthinkable only a decade and half ago. The explanation offered are also very surprising, offered in two parts: one is that Japanese were never able to re-configure or constitute their national and cultural identity as modern Japanese and then, what is even more surprising, that even the widely held images (of very esoteric and very Japanese (unlike its Asian neighbors like Korea or China) in their own highly sophisticated Japanese Oriental ways) had been artificially concocted specifically to cater to Western Orientalism.[54]

In recent decades, it came to light that the Harvard-trained humanistic scholars (led by who else but the great Edwin Reischauer of Harvard) extended legal absolution to a band of Japanese scholar-warriors for their proven war-criminal activities as the Chief of Ideological Warfare for Japanese Fascism cum Militarism in the first half of the twentieth century—yes, I'm here referring to the likes of Nishida Kitaro, DK Suzuki and their former students and colleagues of the so-called Kyodo School of Zen (Samurai Zen) Philosophy. Needless to say such willful rewriting of Japanese history of modernity via Westernization, lock, stock and barrel, perpetrated by the Powers-that-be of American Academic establishment is just another proof of the real and potential threat posed to the future of American democracy and individual freedom of American citizens by what the then retiring President of USA, Dwight Eisenhower made famous in his now famous speech –namely, that of Military-Industrial-Academic Complex, working hand-in-pocket, exercising immense power no one had given them. Their exercise of great power in secrecy, behind the scenes, had never been through any sort of legitimate democratic-political processes, certainly not through popular votes, unhindered any sort of public scrutinizes; they are faceless, invisible, working strictly in secrecy, behind the scenes. The exercise of their unhindered great power is solely derived from the money and the class of super-moneyed controls everything, while the elected public officials remain mere puppet-like figure-heads, a kind of hired hands to represent the vested interests of the moneyed --their corporate and financial interests. In book after another brilliant book after still others, Noam Chomsky has been exposing and critiquing this state of democracy in America with moral passion and genuine concern for the future of the humanity compromised and taken hostage by the shadow powers of the

---

[54] Patrick Smith, *JAPAN: REINTERPRETATION*,.1998.

super-moneyed[55]. The Harvard scholars who had absolved Japanese War Criminals in their audacious act of "historical engineering" (in Chomsky's perspicuous terminology) were doing it, compromising their scholarly integrity and forever corrupting Humanistic Ideals of a modern University, as a bona-fide members of the Power Elites as legitimate full Partners of the Greatest Firm ever in the world history in the name of the great U.S. Military-Industrial-Academic Complex. Otherwise, if not as full partners of this great complex, partaking in the exercise of power to reshape the entire world in the ideological vision of Americanism (cum technopianism), the Harvard Professors of History and Other Area Studies would not have had the access to the dominant hegemonic Power-that-be and be able to absolve the war-criminal activities of the Ideological Warriors of Japanese Fascism cum Militarism –i.e., the likes of Nishida Kitaro, DK Suzuki and others of the Kyodo School of Zen Philosophy.

Those Harvard Professors were in turn the intellectual *eminence grises* in an undeclared Ideological Warfare –therefore, merely a cold war or silent war or an invisible war it had been until the Marx-Leninist Block Ideological Camp's self-immolation around the year 1990-- to spread Americanism cum Technopia to the rest of the world. So concerned about it that Martin Heidegger, this profoundly thoughtful man, mistook National Socialism of Hitler and friends as a potential Third Way, when neither Bolshevism of Marx-Lenin nor Americanism were viable options to take, taking them both in reality to be the same forces of the Planetary Technological Domination in two different faces.

Is Art immune from such a matrix of the calculus of International Power politics? I think not. I have in fact already indicated that the generators (or the authors) of Post-historical, Postmodern, Neo-avant-garde, multiculturalism, Pluralism, etc. from the Cultural-Power Centers of New York and also possibly from London and Paris as secondary Centers could be looked upon as the art-cultural ideological warriors for the spread and domination of American hegemony in all spheres of human endeavors. Pop Art celebrates one form of life, but it is an artificial kind of life industrially constructed *in toto* and run, which can hardly be called human form of life in the way Wittgenstein used the term when he said famously that "to imagine a language is to imagine a form of life." Likewise, to imagine Pop Art a la Warhol is to imagine an industrially constructed artificial form of life in which a human-being qua spiritual being has been eliminated by some shady means in much the same way the cattle and chicken and other animal lives have been totally transformed their very animal nature into an altogether new ontological species –a monster in fact that just looks the same as the traditional cows, pigs and chicken, but they are mere pretenders, their animal nature of being cow seriously compromised by the way they are fed and raised) of mere *industrial raw material in reserve* for mass production and mass consumption. Heidegger had foreseen this eventuality long before Farm Industry, Cattle Industry, Chicken Farms, Food Industry have become realities, spear-headed by American Industrial and Entrepreneurial ingenuity in their religious zeal to remake the planet in its entirety into one giant Machine, everything else on the planet as raw material for industrial production, as a huge technological system, self-run.

Back to the notion of "daam" and "daamhua"

After a digression on Japanese version of Zen experience of Absolute Nothingness for its conceptual vacuity and ideological misuse as a false representation of genuine Seon(禪) experience. We suggest that the key to understanding Seon experience is daam (淡) and jeong(瀞) rather than the notion of 空 (empty), especially, the notion of absolute emptiness in Japanese version. "Daam"

---

[55] PP.44-45,   Korean translation of Patrick Smith, *Japan: Reinterpretation* as 일본의 재구성 일본의 *재구성*

refers to a mood of an ontological kind as in Heidegger –the mood of serenity, utter calmness with no emotional turmoil. In other words, it is about the state of mind and emotion in which all the complex calculus of private, personal interests have been let-go, suspended for a while, so to speak. All those concerns are let settled at the bottom just like a turbulent body of water in a pond becomes still and all the impure elements such as dirt and other matters settle down at the bottom of the pond, making the body of war clear and transparent and then everything in that pond becomes visible, knowable. In the state of mind stilled like a stilled body of water, you'd be able to encounter things for what they are in their own thing-ly nature. I use the 'encounter', because when we're in the state of daamness, we are able to, not a grammatical subject, but as this whole existent being-- Heidegger called DASEIN-- opens up, by letting go of every other concerns both bodily, of the mind, of the soul, or whatever else, and unconsciously (not intentionally) –naturally—respond and interact with any one thing (whether sentient or not) in nature or in the world.   This sort of an encounter is something that occurs spontaneously and unexpectedly between any two things in nature, neither side as a subject or as an object.

Because we're introducing of utterly novel term of 'daam' or 'daam-daam' from Korean language, it may be necessary to find at least one other means of its explication. I want to clarify this concept once again, this time in terms of much better and widely known concept of Myeongsang (瞑想) whose English translation would be somewhat like 'Meditation'. I, for one, think that it is a misleading translation, for Myeongsang is a noun, resulted not as the nominalization of the verb "myeongsang-hada"(to meditate). To mediate is for the mind to actively-- albeit in calm, thoughtful way-- to think about or on certain thing(s). Therefore, to meditate is one of the species of human acting called 'Yinwui'(人爲), willful or intentional acts. Myeongsang, on the hand, is a state of mind that cannot be achieved in any such artificial, willful way. You cannot try, strive or struggle in order to achieve that state of mind of being utterly *calm(靜)* settled in its serenity –the state of being settled in its serenity is exactly the state of 'daam' as we earlier compared it to the state of the body of water in a lake or pond, once turbulent with rain, bring up all kinds of dirt and other impure stuffs, making waves, but after a while, no more inflow and the wind having died down, the body of water is stilled, every other stuff settled down at the very bottom and the water surface calm like one huge piece of glass, transparent.

There can be many different ways of 'myeongsang-hada'(to meditate) and do certain series of actions or take certain actions with your mind as the guide. That is how you're taught to meditate at the many, ubiquitous Meditation Centers and Yoga Studios in any major Metropolitan Cities of the Western World. So, you'd practice these actions in order to arrive at the state of *'myeongsang'*; but these actions have nothing to do with *'myeongsang' itself*. There cannot be artificially assembled curricula the completion of which will take you to the state of Myeongsang –the state of daamness. In Korean Suhaeng tradition, too, the word to "study" is employed when we practice sitting, breathing and other seemingly bodily exercises, some of them designed by former masters, but only as something you may try out yourself in your discovering the one just right only for you, not as a standard fare for everyone; that is to say that in this study of Suhaeing, there cannot be a universally valid program of study for every anyone, something like a tried and proven standard textbook. Each seeker *and suhaeng-ja* (修行人) must discover, independently, what is just right for him or her, because every human being, in the conception of the things in that *Suhaeng* tradition, is unique much in the way no two stones are exactly the same. In the universe, only industrially manufactured goods can be the same. This observation has a profound ramification in a critical and deep understanding of the nature of technology and technologically designed and assembled society.

At this point, let me put forward a thesis: Daamhua Artists are those whose artistic-creative process is nothing like a programmatically pre-established matrixes of actions to take. Especially important point is that Daam Painters do not pre-compose, make a model, or any such things beforehand. In ancient Northeast Asian thoughts, such a methodical way doing things, each step of the way carefully composed, designed, modeled and thus intended, has a name: it is *'yin-wui'* (人爲) or equivalently *'jak-wu'* (作爲); it is that a human agent do it or act it **willfully** with **intention**.

The opposite of willful or intentional human acting is called *'Muwui'* (無爲)*,* which means simply 'not to act' or 'not to do' anything at all: you accomplish doing something by doing nothing' in literal translation. Such a species of acting (doing) is simply not coherent from the perspective of Western philosophical theory of action. Yet, I wish to insist that in all sincerity that this is the very Way of Art-ing (doing art) for these Daamhua Painters from South Korea –theirs is Art through non-arting (無爲藝術). *How to make sense other than as an art which emerges by itself, through his whole body, mind and soul (the holy trinity) as a single medium, so to speak. If one were to video-tape the actual work-process of a daamhua painter, what you'll notice is that he or she seems to move his hand with a brush, moving not by conscious choices but more or less automatically, as if something other than his or her mind guiding his hands and bodily movements.*

Such is the case with a Shaman Dance, for example; the dancing Shaman is not moving according to any sort of pre-choreographed routines. The Shaman might be moving his body this way, that way, while singing as well with not his or her own voice; we say the Shaman dances and sings, guided by an invisible, another force, call it 'spirit'. So, you cannot say that the Shaman in dancing while being possessed by a spirit other than his or her own. The whole artistic piece of dance and music emerged through her, as it were, by itself, automatically: the dance and music just happened, somehow released in the Shaman Dancer as the site (of its occurrence, revelation, happening). Perhaps, one could say the Daam Painters are the Artists who do Shaman-like dance with paint brush in their hands, except that they're not possessed with Shaman spirits but are painting while they're in a state of daamness of his or her mind, body and soul. They are **Artists (藝術家)** as *Daam-Suhaeng-ja (淡修行者).* Of the daamhua painters who're represented here, Kim Chunsoo's Paintings can be explained only in such terms as what I just sketched. I believe it'd be wrong to call his a species of what Harold Rosenberg called some of American Abstractionist Painters as Action Painters. True, he and his followers made vague references to some traces of 'chance' in their Action Painters' works, however even the element of 'chance' pre-planned as to where in the over-all composition it's going to be operative; then, of course, roughly at the same time as Rosenberg, John Cage came up with the so-called 'aleatory music' (*aleatory* from Latin alea, "dice") in which chance or indeterminate elements are left for the performer to realize.

As its Latin root of 'alea', meaning 'dice', indicates, the source of Cage's philosophy of music is, if it is philosophy at all, from the Ancient Northeastern Asia's classical cannon of *Yi-Ching (易經)* in the divination practice of which the dice-like bamboo sticks are used. However, what Cage and other Western artists -- who claimed they were inspired by East Asian philosophical thoughts to be found in the aforementioned *Yi-Ching*—failed to realize was that such 'taking chance' with dices is not just any random acts; it was to be done at the moment of stillness or daamness of his whole being (not just of his or her mind, but the whole existent being of all three of the body, mind and soul are united as one and in that state of serenity of daamness) when that whole-existent being can be in free and spontaneous resonance with anyone thing (sentient or not) in the universe. To act without acting, to do art without ***art-ing***: this 'Mu-Wui'(無爲) Art can be only by a ***Suhaeng-ja***. They don't have Sunhaeng-base culture in the West; again, the central importance of the Suhaeng-aspect of authentic Northeast Asian culture has not been properly appreciated; in fact, even in Northeast Asian countries, that ancient legacy of Suhaeng culture has been forgotten more or less completely.

Not only Cage but other New-age-type Western Artist movements that followed in succession, one after another, when the Nihilism began to overtake the Western World—in the name of modernism and soon infecting the rest of the world-- in spiritual desolation and moral decay, masquerading its true nature (of most cynical nihilistic nihilism) in the most glossy materialistically opulent guises. Theirs is, thus, based upon shallow and erroneous understanding of East Asian thoughts, on the par with the worst case of the fashionable 'new age' spiritualism, proving that the most advanced forms of Arts of the hegemonic centers of the Western Art World are engaged in fraudulent posturing of no substance, whether their movements are named as 'Happenings', 'Fluxus', 'Conceptual Art', 'Performance Art', 'Installation Art' or 'Earth Art'.

It also should be pointed out, I was given to understand that it is only in South Korea, neither in China nor in Japan, a small contingent of Suhaeng culture has been preserved, in secrecy as it were, having been suppressed by Yi-dynasty Chosen Kingdom for their being independent from Han-Chinese Cultural norms within a scholastic and rigidly formulaic ideological reconfiguration of Ancient Northeast Asian Thoughts in the acts of willful transmogrification of those wisdom of Suhaeng-based ancient culture. (That kind of theoretical-philosophical adulteration was necessary to keep the expansionary dynamic of an Empire of Han China; hence the need of the Empire to suppress any ways of life or learning or culture not easily co-opted such as the Suhaeng culture.) Another proof for that tradition of Seon-gar Suhaeng tradition being preserved in almost secrecy for all those more than two or three thousands of years or even more is the proven fact that only in Korea the authentically traditional healing practices are available in accordance with their own very unique philosophical understanding of human body, which is no longer available either in China or Japan, more or less expunged in toto during their heavy-handed modernization of their nations from top-down. Furthermore, in healing practices, the proof is the result of healing which cannot belie any body's eyes.

A new Genealogy of Korean Daamhua Painting is drawn:

Although we dismissed the claims, made mainly by Lee U-fan and Park Seobo as chief spoke persons and leaders of an allegedly indigenously emerged Modern Art movement of 'Korean Monochrome Painting' and then recently Yoon Jin-seop in Seoul suggested calling it 'dansaekhua' (a literal Korean translation of Monochrome Painting) and Joan Kee in USA conferred it another moniker, 'tansaekhua'(again a literal translation of Korean words with slightly different transcription from Yoon's). I disagree with all of these notables of Korean art world for 'much ado about nothing'. There's no such thing as an indigenous movement of Korean monochrome painting as such. They're either a species of the Western modernist painters who did monochrome painting or some who were grouped together under the above monikers but have done art, intrinsically different from what is widely known as art in its global usage within the purview of the Western understanding of 'Contemporary Art'.

There's a very simple criterion for distinguishing above two groups among all those who were classified, falsely as it were, variously as 'Korean Monochrome Painting', 'dansaekhua' a la Yoon Jinseop or 'tansaekhwa' a la Joan Kee. Paintings of authentic and genuine East Asian Art are radically different from the very conception of art and their practices –i.e., ***'arting'*** in my coinage. To make the matter simple, I shall just quote Francois Jullien on this point: "Instead of constructing an ideal Form that we then project on to things, we could try to detect the factors whose configuration is favorable to the task at hand; instead of setting up a goal for our actions, we could allow ourselves to be carried along by the propensity of things. In short, instead of imposing our plan upon the world, we could rely on the potential inherent in the situation."[56] Or, again, "The difference between Western and Chinese thought: one constructs model that is then projected on to the situation, which implies the situation is momentarily 'frozen'. The other relies on a disposition that is known to be constantly evolving."[57]

If a work of painting emerged from authentically Northeast Asia's ancient spiritual and cultural resources, then it has to be an 'art from non-arting' or a Mu-wui(無爲)Art. If any painter begins with a pre-planned model, composition or even a rough sketch, and then work on it by enlarging, adding color and texture and so on, just like building begins with a design in concepts, the miniature model-building and then actual building on a real-world scale; then he is painting as a Western Artist and he or she are fundamentally barred from the spiritual and philosophical sphere of what is distinctly Northeast Asian of the ancient times. Applying this criterion, it is easy to classify both founders of Korean monochrome art movement –Park Seobo and Lee U-fan—as painting as Western Modern or Post-modern, as the case may be, Artists. I understand that Park Seobo carefully in minute detail composes in his sketch book the basic design of his painting and then have a team of his assistants work on it on a large scale. That is essentially the Western Way, very contrary to the Way (道) and Spirit (精神) of East Asia. However, I do think he has surpassed Western Painters as having produced a body of works that are genuinely creative achievements.

Likewise, with Lee U-fan .In his own video-tape, up-loaded over www.youtube.com his personal work process as an Artist, in which he was painting, or rather drawing, using a very fine ink brush called "SePill"(細筆), big ink-brush stroke called 'Hoek'(劃) in an act of representing an objectified Hoek, which should be already and always in movement as a Vector with a direction and energy-force. In contrast to Lee U-fan, another very prominent Asian Painter, Tan Swie-Hian of Singapore, actually wields a giant brush with which he does a kind of Ghi-motion(氣動作) as a Martial Artist might cut the air with greatly concentrated mighty force with a thrust of his arms and fingers forward or sideway, making an invisible but nevertheless real turbulence of ghi-energy flow. (Just consider that a feeble wave of even feebler energy-force made by a butterfly winging may in a very fortuitous occasion might become a hurricane by the time it reaches Gulf Coast of Texas from Amazonian Jungle.) There're other equally important reasons for my classification of him as a Western Artist just like Park Seobo whose art has nothing to do with authentic East Asian spirit and understanding of Art. It is understandable how and why the high-income art critics of the International Art Metropolis like New York and Paris are so easily mistaken about the real nature of his Art; what do they know about East Asia, especially that part of its culture being founded upon Suhaeng not only as a devotee but Suhaeng as a set of basic principles and attitudes and mind set of the people in the practical contexts of their everyday lives. (I've discussed Lee U-fan's Art in connection with Nishida already many paragraphs and pages ago.) Just like, Lee U-fan is a brilliant, clever and successful Western Artist, practicing Art squarely within the game rules of Western' complex of art practices' to borrow Danto's terms.

Modernism in East Asian Art cannot follow the same evolutionary logic of Western Art History. East Asian Artist had and has a choice to be acculturated into a completely Western man in terms of his sensibility, language, cultural demeanor and all that. He then would be able to speak with the

---

56 Francois Jullien, *A Treatise on Efficacy*, University of Hawaii Press, p. 16
57 Jullien, ibid. p. 189

grammar of a Western language and he'd be doing art again with Western cultural grammar, so to speak. They are for all practical purposes Americanized or Westernized men and women, masquerading as Koreans, Chinese or Japanese; but, then, nearly all the populous of contemporary world have become *that* in reality, basically living a quasi-American Ways of Life, dressing and eating pretty much same products from Americanized farm industry, meat industry, clothe industry and all that. It is for this reason that to find a smaller band of Artists who have been able to somehow resist the universal trend of Americanization in all different spheres of cultural life. These are heroes and they're Daam Artists from South Korea, keeping the seed of fire for one day to reignite the dying fire of spiritual life of the humanity.

If Korean art establishment looked upon Park Seobo and Lee Ufan as the leading lights of Korean Monochrome Painting, as Western Modernist Painters, they failed to articulate Korean Modernism in Art, even while making extraordinary contribution to Western Contemporary Art the kind of which their Western Counterparts would not be able dream of achieving. However, their unique geniuses in such brilliant achievements at what they did is on a par with what Conrad did in English Literature, writing in a language which is not his mother tongue. I have no intention of under-appreciating their not insignificant international achievements; their singular achievements is a new species of cultural products, the likes of which can be thinkable only within a historical context of traumatic cultural confrontations between incommensurable ones: the extreme manifestation of which was cultural and spiritual breakdown from which the offspring are still suffering in Central and South Americas, having inherited the unfortunate legacies from their ancestors who were on the receiving ends of the traumatic encounter of half a millennium ago. The drama of cultural confrontations on a planetary scale has not stopped unfolding; Sam Huntington's does show an acute historical insight at least in this regard, the continuous unfolding of Culture-Wars in the guises of the 'Clash of Civilizations' a la Sam Huntington.

In our new Genealogical Tree of Korean (not Western) Modernist Painters, it is Lee Ungno, Yoon Hyeonggeun and possibly Nam Kwan and maybe JH Hah and M Choi as well who must be counted among the First Generation Daamhua Painters of Koreanish Modernism. (I must confess, other than Lee Ungno and Yoon Hyeonggeun, I have not had the time to study the others in any depth yet.) In other words, in place of *Park Seobo* and *Lee U-fan*, I suggest that the true indigenously-emergent Korean cultural modernism as manifested in Art must number *Lee Ungno* and *Yoon Hyeonggeun* as the pioneers. They represent the best of Daamhua Painting "Complex of Art Practices" to borrow Danto's term for Arting Paradigm. Lee Ungno and Yoon Hyeonggeun have been able to demonstrate by exemplification that Korean cultural modernism cannot be the kind of a second-hand or even a second-hand of another second-hand import as from the West via Japan as in the cases of Lee Ufan and his friends. (They re-imported second-hand what the Japanese had imported imperfectly from the West. Even if it was a Nishida or DK Suzuki who played the role model for him, both with highest reputations in Japan and elsewhere, it didn't occur to Lee Ufan that his Japanese Masters might have not have been able to critically partake and act as the most honest cultural and spiritual intermediaries in the cultural transactions from the West to East Asia and also from East Asia to the West, ending up presenting false East to the West and false West to the East.)

The story of Yoon Hyeonggeun and Lee Ungno: they are the figureheads of Korean Daamhua Painting; in their hands, the ancient East Asian complex of art-practices have been reconfigured as East Asian modern art, but 'art' understood totally differently from what is widely understood by that term, standing apart from the History of Western Modern Art in its very inception and conception. What I say East Asian modernism, I mean that they are practicing art in the same way as their ancient ancestors had practiced in that to do art as a daam-Suhaeng-ja (the one who does something like rigorous regiment of meditation and is capable of achieving the state of daamness, of utter stillness, momentarily suspending, or letting go of any and every concerns of body, mind and soul). To Art for them is no different from doing Suhaeng with another means. Furthermore, in their art, it is not any sort of beauty or sublimation they pursue in their artistic creative practices. On the contrary, they wish to paint a daam painting full of daamness—appearing colorless, no drama, insipid even, or possibly even bland. Practicing art in a state of daamess, they create, by not creating with any sort of intentional series of premeditated actions, creating a work that impart daamness. What's the point?

Ancient East Asian Painting—this term, 'painting' is of course not quite appropriate to refer to what the ancient East Asians practiced and produced—is done with brush and ink, never oil. They also never work on stretched canvas. Instead, they used rice-paper or dokk paper which can be as enduring and plastic as any material the Western Artists traditionally used. The stone-ground ink for ancient East Asian had the water-like fluidity. At first, they used ink-brush to write Chinese Ideograms which are composed of individual *Hoeks (劃)*. The thing is, you don't write a Hoek the way you write with your pen on a piece of paper. Hoek is a movement not just of your hand holding the brush but using your entire body in intense concentration and with a motion of your hand into which the entire energy and force of your body is channeled. It is exactly like a martial art movement with your leg, arm or hand; each movement is a forceful vector, making impact on the qi-energy field of your surrounding while invisible but still really there in the sense of being immanent, naturally their -- of nature, out of nature, that is.

Chinese Ideograms being Pictograms, symbolic but also representational, the use of ink brush to write ideogrammatic characters is already to paint, so to speak. Writing with ink brush ideograms like Chinese or Korean Hangeul Alphabet which are also composed of Hoek is none other than painting. [Writing (書)] = [畫 Painting]. Notice the similarity of two characters—nearly identical, in fact. It is wrong to call East Asian Writing with Ink Brush as Calligraphy, for writing with ink brush Hoek by Hoek and give it a configuration of your special kind, as your brushing motion will be done your own force, intensity, rhythm, hesitation, and all that. To write a character with ink-brush Hoeks each of which are vectorial movement with direction and force is to give a unique kind of configuration, thereby creating an invisible force field formed in that particular relationships you had given to the shape. It is nothing other than the latent potential force in Physics, which is not also detectible, unless it is activated. So, the Art of Ink Brush Painting is just the Ink Brush Writing and what is essential in this Art is that it is invisible. The potential is given, conferred by the Artist and now it is up to the viewer who chances upon it to activate the now merely latent potential force and have a feeling of mutual resonance at the level of abstract qi-energy wave mechanical interaction of matter wave to another matter wave coming together either in consonance or in dissonance. Ink Brush Writing is a mere pretext when it is presented as an Artistic Product, it should be considered as a work of Abstract Art. To look for some representational or symbolic meaning would be totally off. So, it is not an Art for every any man or woman; it is done by a Sunhaeng-ja and it can be understood by another Suhaeng-ja. During the Golden Age of Ancient East Asia of 東夷 Dong-yi People (not the ancestors of Han-Chinese but the ancestors of Koreans, Manchurians and Mongolians, the people who then occupied the Central Plains of today's Han China, until they were pushed out from the Center); every any body was a Suhaeng-ja, their culture based upon single most important occupation of Suhaeng which is at the same time a bodily and spiritual exercises.

East Asians didn't have to discover Abstract Painting as the Western Modernist Painters had to in order to rigorously question and interrogate their inherited cultural tradition in an act of historical deconstruction of Heideggerian Epochal thinking in their desperate last effort to reconstitute their rapidly breaking-down cultural convention as a form of life and as a last ditch defensive move to preserve their humanity, especially human spirituality without which their very humanity would self-destruct and morph themselves into a monster with a human face only. The Western Modernist efforts of desperation failed eventually, ending up in the state of the End of Art. Danto, Hal Foster, Cavell and any number of Luminaries in Contemporary Western Cultural Establishment either fails to recognize or wish to turn blind eyes to a historical reality the entire Western World must confront as it is their historical destiny. So, Danto thinks what passes as Contemporary Art, a globe-wide phenomena is proof enough of the solidity and health of Western Modern Civilization they've built and proud of. The voracious Powers that be of their world is capable of co-opting any and everything; it only takes money and a token membership into their midst.

Lee Ungno was able to devise ways of making use Western Maiere of Art to practice an Art of his ancient East Asian Ancestors. He is probably the very first artist, roughly at the same time independently of one another to come up with ***Munja(文字)Chusang(抽象)***Painting. Theirs is a significant artistic achievement that must be given due recognition in the annals of Global Art or cultural history. They have not been given due recognition by the generators of contemporary art discursive practices, being comfortably ensconced in the Centers of Western Modern World they've constructed and dominating from their hegemonic center cities of the West, giving only stingy and token recognitions to artists from elsewhere, practicing art that is different from what they consider to be the most Advanced Art of our time. I know at least one worthy descendent of his school of painting –Park Jonggi and Ahn Jeong-hyeon whose works are represented in this ICA show.

As for Yoon Hyeonggeun, a widely respected but not as well-known as Lee Ufan or Park Seobo; neither are his paintings priced as high as the other two. When you first come upon Yoon's paintings, your first impression might be that some of his paintings look superficially similar to Mark Rothko or Barnett Newman, as duly noticed and written about by critics from inside and outside of Korea. If Clement Greenberg had a chance to look at these paintings, he might have been tempted to apply the same assessment he made of the Japanese painters' abstract expressionist paintings to these Korean painters like Yoon and Choi Myeongyoung, not only to Lee Ufan or Park Seobo. His assessment, however, would have been wrong in the cases of the former, for they were not painting from within the art-historical contexts of the West. The artistic problematic they were grappling with were something entirely different from the one that the Western abstract expressionists were engaged with. Yes, their works were abstract paintings too; but they arrived at their kinds of abstract works from an entirely different point of departure. Yoon was trying to achieve what is uniquely East Asian conception of artistic ideal, using different brush techniques and material. The only thing he shared with Western Abstract expressionist artists' matière was the rectangular-shaped canvas, and even there their canvas was not a stretched canvas-fabric.

In Orient, at least in the Northeast Asian (東北亞) nations of China, Korea and Japan, it is not unusual to talk about the force-field configuration of a mountain range or a terrain in terms of *"hsi"* (勢). The great French Sinologist/Philosopher, Francois Jullien takes this notion of '*hsi*' as the central concept in delineating Chinese world view, as distinct from the Western world view.[58] Just as Chinese Calligraphy is not really about ***writing*** as such, but it is all about ***hsi*** configuration, brought to life, in the way the Artist-Calligrapher uses his brush strokes in his writing. If Western Abstract artists' works are deeply moving, it is so only against the historical backdrop of the destiny of Western Easel Painting-- on its way to its END. Theirs represent brilliant moments just before their imminent death – the End (of Art) in the parlance of Arthur Danto and Hans Belting. With Yoon and other Damhua Painters, their works, in spite of surface resemblances to their Western counterparts, their works do not represent that bitter-sweet moment of any fateful death or any sort of metaphysical end. On the contrary, theirs are rooted in Oriental spiritual and philosophical soil, only now waking up and opening up a new horizon. This is so, because Yoon and his colleagues in their

---

58 Francois Jullien, *The Propensity of Things,* Zone Book, MIT Press

own ways devised ways to make use of the usual material for Western Painting., such as Canvas, Oil and etc. in pursing, as a way of re-defining or re-structuring some aspects of their inherited traditional ways of *Arting* (art-practices), while keeping traditional Oriental Ideal of *Arting* of their Ancestors. ***In a way, these Daamhua Painters are at last the first formulators of Eastasian Modernism in Painting.*** Call it ***neo-modernism***, if you will. As the rediscovery of Ancient Greek thinking –fortiori, also the Great Greek Art— had enabled the West to re-configure the then existing Culture under Church domination and therewith awaken the West's creative energies, hopelessly mired in abysmal blackness of the West's Dark Age; this time at the very beginning of the Twenty-first Century, a band of South Korean Artists are re-configuring the dominant global-wide arting of "Contemporary Art" in a post-historical period. This, then, is nothing less than, nothing other than, Eastasian renaissance on its way to "neo-modernism" that will enable the West and Americanized non-West to flee from the Western-made Nihilist Quagmire of blackest pits.

In other words, this band of South Korean Painters were able to respond to the deeply pained call of Paul Ricoeur, the great French Philosopher in the late 1950s, just when the universal phenomenon of Americanization in the name of modernization was picking up its speed. We see very different interpretive attitudes in Paul Ricoeur's and Danto's responses to that historical phenomenon (of the universal Americanization of modernity); Ricoeur is apprehensive about it, whereas Danto is celebratory, in his celebration of Pop Art as the Apotheosis of Americanism cum Technopianism. It is interesting to note that roughly at the same period, South Korean Painters like ***Lee Ungno***, new arrived in Paris and ***Yoon Hyeonggeun*** in Seoul, whose citizenship newly restored after a long imprisonment, have each in his own way began to Paint (investigate in the act of painting) as a resistance to that universal historical forces of the time. The results of their lonely efforts of Artistic Resistance are Damhua Paintings, whereas Lee Ufan and Park Seobo got on the bandwagon of that Americanized as Monochrome Painters, failing to discover their Eastasian Ancestors' distinct Art World of Daam (淡)Modernism

Notwithstanding critics' and other Art World cognoscenti's inside and outside Korea remarking about the resemblances his works seems to bear to such American painters as Mark Rothko and Barnet Newman as a praise; when looked at from a perspective different from the ones that are present in the typical Modernist and Contemporary discourses from the Western hegemonic centers; it is readily apprehensible that Yoon does something totally different from his Western counterparts as well his Korean colleagues in the same KNMMA exhibition of 'Dansaekhua'. And that is what is so tantalizing; so, similar, yet the artistic and spiritual substances inherent in their works, so radically different. Yoon has always told anyone willing to listen that the immediate genealogy of his painting harks back to the calligraphic art of Kim Jeonghee, the great Korean scholar, calligrapher of two centuries ago. Yet, no Korean and foreign art critics took up that fundamental premise of Yoon's art in their writings about Yoon's art. No art critic knew how to begin to untangle that Zen Koan like statement by Yoon about his Painting's immediate kinship with Chinese Calligraphy of Kim Jeonghee's particular style. The difference between Yoon's and Mark Rothko's works is just like the difference in somewhat similar way Verlaine's poetic substance differ from Su Shi (or So Donpa) in spite of their similar poetic effects of "blandness", as Francois Jullien has so brilliantly pointed out.[59]

Yoon Hyeonggeun's 'Koan' – a Riddle: The key to understanding Yoon Hyeonggeun's Daamhua Painting must begin with a cultural hermeneutics of Yoon's **koan** or ***hwadu***):

> *"The Point of Departure for my Art is Kim Jeonghee's writing".*
> *(In a personal conversation to me just before his untimely death in 2009)*

---

[59] Francois Jullien, ***In Praise of Blandness***,

Don Judd, one of the first Minimalist, together with Robert Morris had a special liking for Yoon Hyeonggeun's abstract paintings; so much so that when Don Judd museum was found near Dallas-Fortworth, Texas, Don Judd changed the architectural design of his museum building in order how best to show-case Yoon's works in his private collection. Why? Judd knew instinctively that such works as Yoon cannot be produced by Western artist, working from within Western Art-historical background, because Western Art was destined for THE END (of Art). Perhaps, I can just explain what I mean by a reference to Hal Foster's recent re-interpretive efforts from his now more mature perspective, presuming to show that Judd or Flavin's literalist art (now Foster accepts the misnomer, an ill-conceived moniker which gave rise to tons of confusion and stupid art-writings such as Lee U-fan or other Japanese equating Minimalist Zen Aesthetics having anticipated Western Minimalism and some such incoherent rhetoric) contains a dimension previously un-noticed, because of the modernist discourses a la Greenberg or Fried; he thinks that Flavin's Light-Fixture installation have spiritual dimension beyond and above the literality of his works. I mean to argue elsewhere that he is entirely wrong; Foster's such interpretation will just be on the par with Danto's celebration of Pop Art. To paraphrase Wittgenstein (Danto approvingly quotes too): to imagine Pop Art is to imagine a form of life not worth living in which preponderant number of the populous will be degraded into happy mass-consumption pigs, devouring fast food as well as fast (and canned) culture and entertainment of no spiritual or intellectual content, while a very small shadowy group of multi-billionaires, allowing no access their consumption human-pigs to any thought of the sheer possibility of an alternative way or ways of life, by co-opting just any everything with a potential discord with the mien of tolerance and generosity, allowing not even any kind of passive resistance. So, if there is any trace of spirituality in Flavin's works of Art, it can only be Las Vegas spirituality of honky-tonk variety-- neo-sign spirituality that is. (Actually, Korea today is the proof to Paul Ricoeur's foreboding that the Universal historical process of Industrialization ad Modernization but that such a national building through economic develop ends with Americanizing their ways of life as well. Today, in Korea, at night you see so many Neon-sign Crosses on Church towers, glittering like stars. Yes, I mean real Churches (that are Christian, of Presbyterian, Methodist, Baptist or whatever denomination) have installed glittering Neon-Sign Crosses, one peculiarity of Korean Christianity; isn't this a proof that Koreans learned well from their American teachers?)

American Art Critics couldn't possibly know what connection there is between spirituality and art. Because, in Anglo-American Philosophical curricula, there're only the first two-thirds of Kant's Critique of Pure Reason on their philosophy students' reading list. They are not asked to read any of the philosophical writings he did in later years (of an old age). They are asked to read, when interested in Aesthetics, Kant's Critique of Judgment; but they are not even told of Kant's quite different views of Art in his other writings. Let me quote what Kant had to say about Art and Spirituality:

> "Art is an expression of the very basic human aspiration towards a perfect community; this aspiration is the ground for the possibility of human spirituality."[60]

I wish to suggest that the notion of 'spirituality' and 'art' in the above quote from Kant comes very close to art as understood and practiced by daamhua painters. Furthermore, all those terms of 'spirituality', 'perfect community' and such can be give conceptual articulations in terms other than those from the traditional Western Philosophy. In daam art, there's nothing transcendental; even man's spiritual aspiration –one of the reasons why humans engage in art—can be give given

---

[60] Quoted in Lucien Goldmann, *Immanuel Kant,*

materialist definition of immanent kind. (I won't be able to do it here other than a mere indication, but will be publishing elsewhere.)

There's another notable historical figure who was concerned with human spirituality of European men of the Post-WWI period; he wanted to rejuvenate human spirituality through art—in his case through his kind of Abstract Painting. Michael Fried said that Kandinsky's painterly project was a failure, not able to paint what is a genuinely abstract painting. It is my judgment that Kandinsky also failed to come up with a conception of spirituality that is realizable through art. (Again, I'll have to make a case for this claim elsewhere.) Heidegger too entertained a similar hope for art to do; for whom, art was an anti-dote to all-enframing thinking of modern technological world view. I say art as an expression of human spiritual aspiration cannot emerge from the Western men the very grammar of their (Western) thinking is not capable of imagining such an art, other than in some transcendental metaphysical terms. It is entirely possible to do Art as an expression of the very basic human aspiration towards a perfect community; that same fulfillment is also the spiritual fulfillment for men. Here, read 'community' as something larger than man or woman, be it a community, nature, universe or even nation, or even such tiny community of just two human beings. Aspiration towards a perfect community simply means the perfect understanding of one another in the sense of attunement (in German, Stimmung) in terms of fundamental existential mood, sensibility or in whatever way –i.e., to be on the same wave length for a harmonic consonant interaction. In ancient East Asian thinking, they call it 'becoming one' with the whole universe, nature, etc. Wave to wave consonance is a material event of actual waves of energy particles of all different sorts; however, for Daam artists, it is qi-energy waves which through their brush works impart onto their canvas and create invisible qi-energy force field as a latent potential and it is this that a viewer responds to visceral – characteristic wave to another characteristic wave. It is possible only when you are able to train your body, mind and soul –your individual holy-trinity—in perfect integration, in working together for all kind of perception, feeling, sensing, understanding or whatever else there might be of cognitive, emotional, intellectual or psychological kind.

*If **Yoon Hyeonggeun's Abstract Paintings of Daamhua** is a sure sign of the birth of a New Art, intrinsically different from what is widely accepted as Art in today's Contemporary Art Scenes;* then there's a further proof that it is not an isolated exception but a genuine new Art movement this time from a non-Western part of the World is to be found in the body of works by ***Kim Taeksang*** whose works are represented here in this ICA Show. His is a genuine exemplar of Light Art much more than Dan Flavin's could hope for, ever. As Hal Foster himself admits, something of a mysterious mood or spiritual mood created by Dan Flavin might be illusionistic effects, creating the illusion of mystical or spiritual mood (or atmosphere) with his literal objects of purchased industrially-manufactured lighting fixtures and/or tubes through the backdoor, as it were. For a card-carrying original member of the first group of Minimalist Artist, counting among them Judd, Robert Morris and himself, his art in whatever form has to be only with literal objects, repudiating any possibility of illusionistic effects. Foster sees the irony, but thinks it might be good thing that Flavin's had that dimension which was previously reluctant to notice and talk about in public, as it might suggest insincerity and bad faith on the part of this artist. Perhaps, Foster got tired of the barren, lifeless, spiritless, gesturing and posturing of no substance in the forlorn landscape of contemporary art (Western Art) in complete desolation, decadence, and spiritually sterile quagmire of nihilism, masquerading it as chic, advanced or sophisticated, ah yes, and then too 'fashionable'.

In contrast to Flavin's false spirituality as false as Korean Churches with Neon-Sign Crosses; Kim Taeksang's works are REAL art, forging authentic works of art of REAL rays of light, not an illusion created through industrial light. It was possible for Kim to create real light emanate from inside of the canvas, so to speak. How is this possible? First, he pays respectful attention to his material –the fabric, the color mixture which he does himself through painstaking research from different plants, vegetable or other natural raw material. Then, he applies the freshly mixed color over the canvas thin, very thin. When dried, he repeats the process, but it is not a mechanical repetition; rather it is an endless process of reiteration. As he doesn't use rulers or mechanical devices to ensure geometrical exactitude, at each new cycle of reiteration, there's bound to be fissures. Through trial and error, he builds up many different thin layers of colors, like putting one color film over another. In such combinations, he creates a work in which the light, the rays light seem to flow out, emanate or stay still in a standing wave packet of the light waves. The light in his work is REAL LIGHT from the sun or in the studio; none of the light effects as in the Science and Technology of Lighting and Light Effects.

On his canvases, Kim Taeksang had created potential light-particle energy field or a structure of sub energy fields an invisible energy field. His can be mistaken as doing Optical Art; but no. He want you to use your sensory organs in its fully alert states in combination of all other sensory organs of your body in perfectly consonant harmony as one; then, you will realize that your eye sights have been unnecessarily limited only one kind of viewing experience. Not filtered through some representational matrix of perception, but have your eyes' sensory organ to respond directly, without thinking, naturally as it were with any one thing in the world, outside you, in an equal relationship, coming together naturally, not as a subject and as an object. If anything, his is as a body of works of art most exemplary of Daamhua Painting. Furthermore, it is in Kim's works that a genuinely a New Spiritual in Art can be said definitely emerging; it is the kind of art that Wassily Kandinsky once wanted to present to the world as an antidote to the pervasive nihilism overtaking the cultural sphere of the West. Kandinsky failed to come up with an Art, a new kind of Abstract Art that will be the art work of *the New Spiritual in Art* the Historical Epoch of his time demanded. (Heidegger too looked to art to play that role Kandinsky had in mind, after all.)   Unfortunately, here is not the time to go any further. I mean to do it elsewhere very shortly, possibly for his October One Man Show at a Gallery in Busan, South Korea.

A Digress: More on Kim Taeksang, A Meister-Painter of Light

Looking at any of his works in this series of Breath Light Paintings, a careless viewer might immediately call them as the works of Monochrome Painting. Or, another might see some resemblance with Optical Paintings of, say, Joseph Albers or even Gotthard Graubner. But he or she would be dead wrong on both counts. On the contrary, these works of painting belong to an entirely different and new species of Painting by the name of Daamhua(淡畵). Before attempting to explain what is meant by this novel term, let us begin with Kim's works and provide a hopefully persuasive case as to how and why these paintings of Kim's are bona fide Daamhua Paintings thereby also explain the meaning of 'daamhua'.

Let us begin with his painting, 'Breath Hue –gently – softly'. Being Paintings on Canvas, they have surely been painted on a flat two-dimensional planar surface (of the canvas). Yet, the very material reality of the work seems to have become dematerialized, leaving only colored Light shyly, every so quietly, shimmering through a rectangular opening, rather than pouring in or out, from somewhere inside, as it were. There's a very quiet, ever so gentle, pulsation of light (in that color spectrum) bundle –hence, the Artist's calling his own works of Painting as that of 'Breathing Light'. So, it doesn't seem quite right to say that these paintings have been painted in color, even though that's what's been done. Rather, it seems more appropriate to say that his paintings have been painted in Light of this or that particular color spectrum, of that hue. When the light fixtures are turned off and therefore in darkness, his paintings of red hue would be just a source of light, ever so mutely and quietly emitting feeble but gently pulsating rays of light. A magic has been done. How is it possible to create a Painting of Light rather than a Painting of Color?

Kim pays special attention to the very materiality of his painterly matière such as the fabric for his canvas, oil and brush for their specific characters. For example, Kim uses a specially weaved textile fabric which has the same water-absorption rate as the traditional Oriental Rice Papers traditionally used for Ink-Brush Painting. Although he uses Acrylic for his color, it is not oil based but water-based to give his painting the overall Ink-Brush type of texture and phenomenological milieu. When Oil-based Acrylic is used, all anyone can paint on a canvas would be pigment color, incapable of adducing the shimmering quality of light-color. The artist researches and experiment on his color mixture, never using industrially produced product but does it himself through a painstaking trials and errors of using all different sorts of plants, vegetable or other natural raw material. Then, he applies the freshly mixed color over the canvas of specially ordered water-absorbent fabric thin, very thin. When dried, he repeats the same process, and then again as in fractal bifurcation onto the next and still the next level ad infinitum. If it weren't for this time-consuming intensive labor, building up thin layer over thin layer to the nth power level, the kind of pulsating, shimmering light color effects cannot be obtained.

Then, too, look closely at his works at this exhibition and you cannot help but noticing a rectangular patch of light shimmering, whose source seems to lie somewhere inside of the painting itself.   What is the source of this mysterious inner light? This is not a result of some color painting. The light does not come from some color patch, applied with brush as in traditional works of painting. The flood of light enveloping the Christ figure you see in Caravaggio's 'Supper at Erasmus' is a result of chiaroscuro he introduced to European Painting for the first time. However great this achievement is for Caravaggio and subsequently for Rembrandt, the effects of the flooding light is a result of a painted illusion. The artistic effects of the flooding light in their paintings are transcendent.

In contradistinction to the illusionistic effects of transcendence, the inner light you notice in Kim Taeksang's works is the result of immanence; in other words, Kim's inner light which seems to radiate from somewhere inside (from some depth down below) is from the natural sources. That's the meaning of IMMANENCE. This is where Kim Taiksang, although he was initially trained as an artist in the style of Western Painting, Kim Taiksang has come full cycle back to his own cultural and artistic root of the Orient. As Francois Jullien so acutely pointed out in his brilliant books (like IN PRAISE OF BLANDNES and THE IMPOSSIBLE NUDE: CHINESE ART AND WESTERN AESTHETICS), traditional East-Asian artists do not aspire to Transcendence as their Western counterparts do; it is IMMANENCE which the traditional Chinese Art wanted to achieve in their artistic effects. So, how does Kim Taiksang achieve this quality of radiating inner light as a result of immanence? Let me explain:

Western method of image-making in representation has always been in terms of a grid structure, finer and finer grid structure making the representation more and more realistic in proportion to the ratio of grid on the canvas to the subject motive of the painting. The grid-geometry as the structuring device is like an all-encompassing net from which there is no escape; there's no leeway or hidden and warped fissure in this structuration. In Kim Taiksang's method of working, his principle of structuration is more in terms of fractal or rhizome-like geometries in the idioms of Deleuze and Guttari (for example, in their co-written books like CAPITALISM AND SCHIZOPHRENIA). In fractal geometry, in further bifurcation at further and further levels of re-iteration of the self-same diagrammatic activities, there're always unexpected nooks and crevices at each newer levels of iteration. Looked upon as a fractal-geometrical structuration in Kim Taiksang's works of building up the many-layered structure of thinly applied water-based acrylic color ink, so to speak; there are many thousands of cracks and fissures (of microscopic spaces) hidden under the carefully piled-up thinly layered structure. Together, these fissures (of microscopic hidden spaces) form the geometry of ground in the figure-ground dialectic. Therein, in the geometry of the grounds (in its relationship to the figures) is latent a configured form of potential force. Onto that potential field of forces the light, whether natural or electric, falls to create an entirely new kind of pulsation, a resonance of the light particles and the captured light particles within certain well-defined color-spectrum of the configured ground. The inner light is THAT pulsation, that resonance, not any sort of color effect at all. It is in this sense that Kim Taiksang's inner light is from the natural sources and hence the light effects in his works are real, immanent, rather than being that of transcendence –that is, of illusion as in the case of Western Optical Painters like Joseph Albers, for instance.

It is in just that sense of the above paragraph that Kim Taiksang's works have nothing to do with post-structural cultural ideology, as Deleuze and Guttari also points out that Fractal thinking has nothing to do with post-structuralism in spite of what poorly-educated cultural critics are wont to lump them (Deleuze and Guttari) among their rank.[61] But, what has to be pointed out is that there's no need to go to Deleuze and Guttari for right theoretical frame work for the hermeneutic exegesis of Kim Taking's works, as what Delouse and Guttery are pointing towards in their critical interpretation of the Western-modern civilization can be, all of them, found in the traditional Oriental Philosophical thinking, when it is done in a truly 'philosophical' way. In recent years, only in recent years, the brilliant French Sinologist/philosopher, Francois Jullien have discovered a way of approach to re-discovering the profound philosophical approaches to understanding of the universe and its process, which are so starkly different from the Western philosophy, especially the version which made modern Western civilization possible. In Fractal geometry, in Chaos theory, however minute, the initial given can make all the difference in the future reiteration of the self-same, with infinite unexpected formations in a series of continuous bifurcation at each newer levels of iteration as in Mandelbrot Set, the best known example of Fractal Geometry, given birth to the idea of "fractal being" in Deleuze's happy coinage (of the term).

As a Magir der Licht, if Graubner is a Magir der Farbe and Albers a Magir der (Optical) Illusion, Kim Taiksang's works remind us of Dan Flavin who is considered to be THE most important Artist of Light in the Western Art World at least since the early 1960s to this day. Flavin is known as one of the very first Minimalist Artists together with Don Judd and Robert Morris, eschewing any trace of representational painterly idiom from their works in its entirety; that's the formal commitment for any card-carrying minimalists. Yet, after more than 40 years, the doyen of American Contemporary Art Criticism, Hal Foster has recently admitted that something of mysterious mood of spiritual atmosphere create -- perhaps unintentionally and for long ignored as if non- existent, in Dan Flavin's works of Light Arts installations—might be illusionistic effects, after all. Well, this is a huge admission, for it goes against the formalist dictum of Minimalist Aesthetics that their (minimalist) art had to do only with literal objects, repudiating any possibility of illusionistic effects. Yet, if Hal Foster is correct, then Flavin can be accused of bad faith and insincerity in his turning blind eyes to what is there to be taken notice of in his own works. Foster sees an irony in this belated noticing or acknowledgement of the presence of illusionistic effects in what were allegedly paradigmatic Minimalist Art Products, using nothing but literal objects of purchased industrially-manufactured lighting fixtures and tubes; yet, as it turns out that he had implicitly brought in illusion through the back door, as it were, unacknowledged. So, the mysterious and even sometimes surreal effects of Flavin's Light shows owed their mystic in the unacknowledged presence of illusionistic effects. It is surprising that Foster doesn't see the potential fissure in the long-held sacrosanct Minimalist Discourse of the Western Centers of Global Art. Until a new discursive framework is put forward to provide a plausible explanation for the fissure as in fact a positive quality in his works; it is just

<hr>

[61] Clearly, this requires further explanation, but it has to wait for the next occasion, this not being the right venue for such a technical discoursing.

another sign of the hubris, hypocrisy, bankruptcy and nihilistic bad faith pervasive in the main-stream art-discourses of the Western Centers.

In contradistinction to Dan Flavin, Kim Taiksang's Art of Light has no such theoretical problems, as he actually creates the shimmering light effects IN REALITY; they're actual rays of light color of that hue, materially created off the surface of his canvas. That is the reason why I called it the Art of Immanence, the sin qua non of ancient East Asian artistic practices in contradistinction to Western Art always in pursuit of TRANSCENDENCE. It is transcendent beauty or sublimity Western Artists wanted to achieve in their works of art. It Western Art is that of transcendence, then genuinely East Asian Art is that of Immanence. Then, too, Kim Taiksang's can be fruitfully discussed in comparison to Joseph Alber's series of works known as "Homage to Square". Through clever maneuvering with perspective and careful juxtaposition of color (whether chromatic [identifiable hues] or achromatic [black, white or gray]) as well as a judicious use (of intermingling) of positive and negative spaces as critically important compositional elements, Joseph Albers created Optical Effects of virtual movement in his Masterpieces of Op Art. However, again, as with Flavin above, Albers' optical effects nothing other than illusionistic trickery in the end, while Kim Taiksang's light effects in real terms without resorting to sort of trickery. That is an achievement enough! Is it not? Flavin would have loved to do what Kim Taiksang has done. Joseph Alber would have, too, for that matter.

Then, too, superficially at least, Kim Taiksang's works resemble the so-called Monochrome Paintings of the West. And, in fact, he was so classified as one of representative Korean Monochrome Painters when Korean National Museum of Modern Art organized a massive exhibition under the title of KOREAN DANSAEKHUA.

However, nothing could be farther than that! This artist is doing something entirely different, as I made it evident in Part I of this essay. Kim Taiksang and his colleagues are taking visual art into an unknown territory, which refuses to stay within or with the history of contemporary painting other than that his are also exhibited in Gallery spaces. In everything else, in the kind of aesthetic effects he pursues and the artistic goal he sets for him are entirely different from the contemporary paradigm of doing-art. He (and likewise for his other colleagues who are also doing arts in painting, in sculpture or whatever else in the style of Daamhua) is unique even among Korean artists, unlike any other. It is perhaps useful to contextualize his works within the brief history of contemporary Korean Art and prevailing milieu of the Korean Art Scene today.

There's an intriguing and provocative passage at the end of a short chapter on Korean history in the standard college text book on the History of East Asia by Craig, Fairbank and Reischauer. The three Harvard Historians had raised this interesting question (in paraphrase): what is it about Korean people that they went to such dogmatic extremes in their appropriation of Neo-Confucian teachings that they thought nothing of killing their opposing factions over some trivial exegesis of a passage in some Confucian canonical texts, over something that is not even their own invention but an import from outside – namely, China? The same question can be raised about Korean people with their ardent embracing of Christianity, while it had no success in proselytizing their next door neighbor, Japanese people. The same kind of fervent embracing of foreign ideas, something that is totally alien to their own spiritual and cultural soil, has happened in Korean contemporary art as well; in this case, and it is the Western idea of 'avant-garde', Nam Jun Paik being only one of the earliest to do so. There's no dearth of his epigones in Korea. It is for some such reasons that Korean artists seem to take much greater pride in having their works at such Western avant-garde venues as Venice Biennale or Cassel Documenta than having their works shown and sold at Commercial Art Auctions. Whereas Korean artists were busy in appropriating the peculiarly Western need for pure 'concepts', not satisfied with dealing in the worldly realm of 'reality' in such Western avant-garde preoccupation with the conceptual art and some other similar bastardized versions of nihilistic posturing, Chinese artists were much more pragmatic even in the way they appropriated Western styles of modern art. Surely, Professor Francois Jullien's brilliant exposition of how different the Chinese philosophical disposition was from the Western men's in their rejection of the world of pure ideas as irrelevant, thus pursuing the 'immanence' rather than 'transcendence'. The contemporary Chinese artists too have appropriated Western avant-garde, but it was with an eye to explore the kind of Pop culture haven that the East Asian societies have become, as a result of economic development accompanied by the modernization of what used to be very traditional societies.

Kim Taiksang's works of paintings shown here are not of the species of (Western) Monochrome Painting. Neither are they of the species of Dansaekhua of alleged Korean or East Asian Modernist Art as opposed to Western Modernism. Rather, they are species of Daamhua Painting, emerging out of Korea. Daamhua is a highly spiritual art. For the Practitioners of Daamhua Painting, Art is a device for Spiritual Connectedness in the sense of what both Chuang-tzu and Kant have said in their own peculiar idioms. (Here, I don't mean the Kant of his peak career but in his late, very late writings in which he seems to reject his earlier ideas of Art and Aesthetics.) Let me explain:

Kim Taiksang's body of works is bound to find a great deal of attention among the spiritually starved post-modern men and women, especially in Europe and North America. (I say, more in the Western World than in Asia, mainly because Asians like South Koreans and the Chinese are still in the middle of economic development and are too busy to accumulate wealth for their nation as well as for their own individual families to pay much attention to their spiritual needs.) My German friend wrote to me that there are more Yoga Studios and Meditation Centers in Germany as well as other countries of European Union than Starbucks Coffee Houses. The same goes for North America, especially in such places as in Northern California, around San Francisco Bay Area. Western-led modernization via scientific-and-technological advances has brought us Material Wealth, something that our ancestors couldn't even dream of. Look around Korea society, and it is easy to see that every fabric of Korean traditional culture has gone through a profound process of metamorphosis. In Korea, too, there's bound to be a gradually increasing awareness on the part of the profit-mongering people that material well-being is no guarantee for happiness. They'll discover that spiritual well-being as well as bodily-health (bodily-well-being) is possibly even more important. And, for these people, awakening to their spiritual needs, Kim Taiksang's works of art will speak volumes, in grabbing their attention, as his works point to the existence of another dimension of life –namely, that of spirituality.

In his later life, near to his death, after having had a chance to look back upon his life's achievement in a grand summing up of the entire spectrum of Western Philosophical tradition, Immanuel Kant had more or less rejected his earlier articulation of the traditional Western Philosophy of Art and Aesthetics in which he is still touted as the greatest. Possibly for that reason, his late laminations of the nature of Art and Human Spirituality have been near-totally neglected in the University curricula. (Well, there's been an exception, as Lucien Goldmann has actually written about this neglected aspect of Kant in his own dissertation by the title of IMMANUEL KANT.) Just consider these tantalizing words from Kant, something the Kant of the period of the Critique of Judgment would not be able to utter: "Art is an expression of the very basic human aspiration towards the perfect community, and this aspiration is the ground for the possibility of human spirituality." Kim Taiksang's ART belongs to this 'ART' and to this 'SPIRITUAL QUEST' in the best Kantian senses of the terms in the above-mentioned phrase of Kant's. It is NOT A SURPRISE that one of the best exemplifications of Late-Kantian sense of Art and Spirituality comes from the body works by Korean Painters such as Kim Taiksang (and his other Daamhua colleagues). For late-Kant, Kant at old age, at least in his laminations on Art and Spirituality in the first chapter of his

INTRODUCTION TO LOGIC, comes close to Oriental Philosophical articulation of Art and Spirituality.

In Kant's saying that "Art is an expression of the very basic human aspiration towards a perfect community," what is meant by the notion of 'perfect community'? It is nothing other than connectedness, connectedness to everything in the universe, to each and every exiting 'beings', be it another human being, a stone, a plant, or an insect such as a Butterfly in Chuang-tzu's Dream(莊周夢爲胡蝶). Notice that Kant uses another adjective to modify the connectedness in the word of 'perfect'. A perfect community and a perfect connectedness: it is what is in Oriental Philosophy usually referred to as 'unity' or 'oneness' (合一).

Discovering 'connectedness' with the Universe, with every ordinary things in the Universe, is a nothing other than 'wonder' and 'joy' when this connectedness has nothing to do with any sort of worldly concerns like profit, self-interest, power-mongering, or any such things. The pure joy of discovering some sort of 'disinterested' connectedness is what Art is all about. Let me explain. We use the verb 'notice' to describe a particular kind of perceptual experience in our ordinary daily lives. For instance, I've been teaching this class for the past three months since the beginning of this new semester. I've been seeing the same faces every day for the past three months. Yet, only now, after three months, I 'notice' this girl, say, "Jiyun" or "Sunyi" or "Youngja". It is not that I did not see her. In a way, I've been seeing her and yet not seeing her until now. That is when I can say, "I noticed her today." What does it mean? Something about her struck me today. In such a noticing, there's an element of 'surprise' and 'wonder'. It is a surprise because she's been there within the field of my vision all this time and yet did not see her. Seeing is more or less mechanical process, bringing to that particular perception of 'seeing' a complex network of our knowledge. As Ernst Gombrich said, 'We see what we know." In other words, in seeing, we bring a software package as our lens and filter the raw sense data out there through our ready-made schemata of perception. However, in noticing, there's been a 'mismatch' between our software scheme and the data out there. Hence, the usual [mechanical] perceptual process of seeing is stopped for a moment; momentarily, we have to reconfigure our software in order to process this mismatch. Since all our pre-established, learned perceptual schemata (software) has been rendered useless and an utterly new perceptual experience of noticing took place OUTSIDE the usual, standard, learned schemata (complex of out wants, interests, prejudices, etc.), the perception is completely DISINTERESTED. Yes, that 'disinterestedness' of Immanuel Kant, as the fundamental condition for aesthetic attitude. Disinterested, here, means 'FREED FROM ALL SORTS OF RULES, CATEGORIAL SCHEMES, CALCULUS OF INTERESTS AND PROFIT MOTIVES."[62] (註: 孔子의 大學에 知止定靜이란 문구가 있다. 지금 우리의 문맥상 중요한 개념은 靜이다. 모든 私的인 욕망, 이해관계에 물려있으면 고요해지지 않는다. 그래서 靜 또는 寂寥의 상태를 이룩할 때 安, 즉 제 모습을 드러내, 慮, 즉 카테고리의 경계와 다른 모든 한계를 넘는 우주적인 사고를 하여 우주와 합일을 이루어 得道할 수 있다고 하였다. 얼마나 이런 동양적 사고에 가까이 왔는가?)

When and if such a noticing occur, one is overwhelmed with a sense of wonder, not because it is some earth-shaking profound something; in fact, it can be something very banal and simple, yet seen in a new light. When something like this happens, the person filled with a sense of wonder HAS TO (it is in human nature to so want) share this experience with another human being by reaching out in the sense of saying, "Do you also see what I see?" It is one of the most modest and sincere gesture one can have towards another person by calling attention of that other person to what he or she noticed. To find WONDER in the most ordinary things, that is Wonder and Joy. In some such

---

[62] 孔子의 大學에 知止定靜이란 문구가 있다. 지금 우리의 문맥상 중요한 개념은 靜이다. 모든 私的인 욕망, 이해관계에 물려있으면 고요해지지 않는다. 그래서 靜 또는 寂寥의 상태를 이룩할 때 安, 즉 제 모습을 드러내, 慮, 즉 카테고리의 경계와 다른 모든 한계를 넘는 우주적인 사고를 하여 우주와 합일을 이루어 得道할 수 있다고 하였다. 얼마나 이런 동양적 사고에 가까이 왔는가?

way, we find connectedness to everyone else and everything else, and this connectedness is completely disinterested, as a result of 'being freed from all pre-established ready-made formulae and schemata". (This is nothing other than 'emptying of our mind' in Oriental Zen tradition.) This is nothing other than momentary enlightenments(覺). In sharing such ordinary wonder in life in universe, we reach a perfect community, in sharing pure sensibilities, freed from all worldly calculi.] Yes, there's a community when there are more than two people. And, this meeting of the minds, this community is established with no thoughts to personal profits, no personal interests of any sorts whatsoever. In East Asian thoughts, this very possibility of 'no thoughts of profit' or the absence of self-interest is called 'haetal' (解脱).[63]

Because, noticing took place without any prior warning, accidentally as it were, and called out to anyone in her vicinity at that moment, spontaneously, 'Do you see what I see?, Can you feel what I feel?" in order to share that pure sense of wonder just for the sake of sharing, just for the sake of 'pure' sense of connectedness as a miniscule part of the same universe.

Now, notice again that 'noticing' takes place in a moment of complete 'disinterestedness', when all desires and emotional excitements have been settled down –i.e., calmed. In the state of 'calmness' and 'settled-down-ness', one achieves the state of daam. Painters of Daamhua are suhaengjas (修行者들) who strives in their daily lives to achieve the state of daamness and their act of painting is also a species of Suhaeng (修行) itself. And, too, the outcome of their Act of Painting As Suhaeng exude the painterly milieu of daamness, making and helping viewers to respond in the same way. Daamness if the one ideal for which all traditional East Asian Arts strove to achieve rather than any sort of Ideal Beauty or something Sublime.

In just in that sense of the term, "daamness", Kim Taiksang's works of painting in this exhibition exemplify the best of daamhua Art. This is nothing other than an emerging New Spiritual in Art for the spiritually starved modern men and women all over the world, emerging from South Korea of all places. It is a new voice of the new Epoch. Let there be light in the future of Daamhua Art on its way to enlighten, to wake the alienated humanity, mired in their addicts life –addicted to fast foods, fast sex, fast this and fast that, all in the throes of technological gadgetry, for fast consumption of any everything. Kim Taiksang's kind of Daam Painting of Light Color rather than pigment color aims to rediscover lost humanity for the lost souls of this contemporary world. After all, at the beginning, there was only Light, the shimmering Light, and nothing else. To become one with light; is this not the ultimate spiritual aspiration of every Man and Woman?

Also: More on Kim Tschunsoo

The very nature of artistic pursuit evident in each of Kim Tschunsoo's Works of Painting is the result of the *deterritorialization of the mindscape*, in fact. First, observe that these works of Kim seem to be the Paintings of *'all-over'* style, reminding one of the 1950s New York Action Paintings. It'd, however, be wrong to impugn such a thing to Kim's works together with 'Action' painting in the referential context of Abstract Expressionism of Jackson Pollack et al. As Michael Fried demonstrated in his catalogue essay on the occasion of exhibition of Three American Painters at Harvard's Fogg Museum already in 1964, Jackson Pollack's *'all-over'* painting was a device or a technique he employed in order to expunge all representational traces from inside the boundaries of his canvases. Again, in Fried's words, Pollack covered every square millimeter of his canvas in such

---

[63] 解脱(haetal) is a Korean Buddhist terminology for 'liberation'. Thus, the road to wisdom is premised upon the liberation of oneself from all worldly desires.

an effort, thus eliminating any possibility of reading spatial depth from his painting, thereby achieving an absolutely *flat* painterly plane, parallel to the literal flatness of his (material) canvas. In other words, it was a *formal* device. This is the point which Harold Rosenberg failed to notice in his discursive development of the so-called 'Action Painting', the notion 'action' having been derived from what was then a very fashionable French Post-WWII version of 'existentialism' in which individual commitment, for whatever cause, whether moral or political, is made and then acted upon with all the passion he or she could muster. That, Sartre advocated, was the only way to combat Nihilism which was an unavoidable existential condition of modern men and women (and he meant 'Western' men and woman) in Post-WWII World; it was, for him, a historical mood, like Pest or some other equally devastating contagious disease, which had infected every living person of conscious minds after the great War that lay the Entire world waste, with the exception of North America.

But, to *act* requires the exercise of one's *Will*, whereby one makes moral or political or aesthetic choices and then it is to act on it that is the important thing with all one's heart, not paying much attention to the result(s) where that action might lead. Likewise, Rosenberg focused on the Act of Painting itself, looking upon the finished painting as only the physical manifestation, a kind of residue, of the actual work. In retrospect, the existentialism of the Post-WWII Western World was just a passing fashion, the philosophical articulation of which turned out to be second-rate misunderstanding of Heidegger's Being and Time (by Sartre), which is of some historical importance to the extent that it reflected the Nihilistic Mood of the time. Likewise, with Harold Rosenberg's interpretation of New York style Abstract Expressionist Painting. All the while Rosenberg placed all the importance to the Act of Painting on the arena of action which is his or her canvas; how that action the painter took in the process of doing his or her painting-act resulted in the final outcome **did matter**, especially, in working within the boundaries of the canvas. First of all, if the sheer act was *everything* and the result nothing but just a record of his panting-act, then there's something insincere about the artists' putting up his works for gallery exhibitions and trying to make living as Artists by taking them to art markets for sales. If they were committed to that conception of *Art-ing* (which is my coinage for 'doing art'), then they should have done it as one among different possible species of Spiritual Exercises for one's own spiritual well-being. Is it not already fraudulent in taking what he or she took to be unimportant -- in being merely a residue of his or her individual spiritually exercise of masturbation-- to the art market? (But, then, it is no different in all areas of commercial transaction in todays' Capitalist Market Places where they laud a Fraud who sells a hip of 'shit' or rotting fish as a bona-fide work of art for 'zillions' as a Genius. How else do you explain the phenomenon of Damien Hearst? Seriously! Or again, how else do you explain the so-called 'financial technology or engineering' that turns junk bonds into suddenly legitimate (hedge) Funds for International Corporate transactions?)

Then, too, there's a problem with Rosenberg's usage of the term, 'action' in 'action paining'. *Action painting* is a style of painting in which paint is *spontaneously* stained, dribbled, splashed or smeared onto the canvas; the surface of the canvas is never carefully composed or designed beforehand, before the application of paint. Yet, all of these actions, the act of dribbling, splashing, etc., require the emptying of the pail of paint, requiring the use of muscle power. Any muscular movement must be directed by his mind, scanning the length and width of the canvas and using muscular power to lift the pail over here and there and pour out the content. To that extent, these actions are guided by the mind, the eye sights and his or her well-coordinated muscular power; it is therefore non-sense to call it *spontaneous acts*. Yes, perhaps, they seem spontaneous or give that impression of spontaneity. But are they? In ancient Northeast Asian thoughts, any human act has a name: it's called *yin-wui (人爲 or 作爲)*, where any 'to do' by a human agent is to do or to act *willfully*, with **intention**. The opposite of willful or intentional human acting is called *muwui* (無爲), which means simply 'not to act' or 'not to do' anything at all. Just in this sense, Rosenberg's followers' vague incantation of 'chance' as in John Cage's so-called 'aleatory music' (aleatory from Latin alea , "dice") in which chance or indeterminate elements are left for the performer to realize. As its Latin root of 'alea', meaning 'dice', indicates, the source of Cage's philosophy of music, if that is philosophy at all, is from the Ancient Northeastern Asia's classical cannon of Yi-Ching (易經) in the divination practice of which the dice-like bamboo sticks are used. However, Cage's and other Western art movements that followed in succession, one after another, when the Nihilism began to overtake the Western World (and soon afterwards infecting the rest of the world) in spiritual desolation and moral decay, were disguising its true nature (of most cynical nihilistic nihilism), masquerading in the most glossy materialistically opulent guises. Theirs is, thus, based upon shallow and erroneous understanding of East Asian thoughts, on the par with the worst case of the fashionable 'new age' spiritualism and as such this is an example of the fraudulence "as the pervasive possibility" (in Stanley Cavell's perspicuous coinage as we had several occasions to quote already in this writing earlier) in the self-proclaimed "the most advanced" forms of Arts of the hegemonic centers of the Western Art World, whether their movements are named as 'Happenings', 'Fluxus', 'Conceptual Art', 'Performance Art', 'Installation Art' or 'Earth Art', or whatever else.

Whether it is in the sense of the formalist conception of **'all-over-ness'** or in the style of Rosenbergian of the **action of painting** all-over the canvas with whatever means or in whatever ways, Kim's is not that kind of 'all-over' painting. Kim's 'all-over-ness' is not achieved in their way of 'paint-acting', nor is his meant to achieve the same kind of formalist rejection of illusionism of all representational traces as in Rosenbergian Action Painting. Well, Kim's way of painting, too, achieve the same formalist consequences as Pollack's 'all-over-ness'; however, it is not what Kim's painting is primarily about, at all. Kim's 'paint-acting' does something entirely different in fact, and if all representational traces are also eliminated from his painterly plane as well, then it is an unintended byproduct of a sort, as it were. In Kim's, there's the deterritorialization of the (familiar) Mindscape, but it is not to construct another mindscape, differently-oriented alternative 'mindscape' with different aesthetic effects as well as affects as in the case of Cezanne. But, if not a mindscape, what then is Kim's works of Painting all about? The answer is simple: it's all about *myeongsang(溟想)*. Let me explain Kim's Painting-Act in a state of *'myeongsang'*:

Meditation is a misleading translation of *'myeongsang'*, for *myeongsang* is a noun, resulted not as the nominalization of the verb *"myeongsan-hada"* (to meditate). To mediate is for the mind to actively, albeit in calm, thoughtful way, to think about or on certain thing(s). Therefore, to meditate is one of the species of human acting called *'yinwui'(人爲)*, willful or intentional acts. Myeongsang, on the hand, is a state of mind that cannot be achieved in any such artificial, willful ways. You cannot try, strive or struggle in order to achieve that state of mind of being utterly *calm(靜)* settled in its serenity. There can be many different ways of *'myeongsang-hada'* and the actions which you do as your mind guides you. You take these actions in order to arrive at the state of **'myeongsang'**; but these actions have nothing to do with **'myeongsang' itself**. What Kim does, as a paint-acting human agent, is not that kind of action, consciously guided by his subjective mind with his will and intention. In other words, his drawing and scratching with a wooden stick, fingers, hands and whatever else are not done **willfully or intentionally**, as it were; rather, his painterly gestures (or perhaps, is 'movements' better term to use?) are in some perfectly consonant dance of a cosmic kind. In other words, his gestures and movements with his hands and fingers have not been choreographed and rehearsed beforehand; they're by themselves coming out of him, automatically as it were, his body as the medium. How is this possible? Let me elaborate this point a little bit further, as it is something difficult to accept for most people who are unfamiliar with these phenomena being described in these terms in these sentences that I am composing now.

Human mind is none other than matrices of images, representational knowledge, other such elements that go to make up one's sight, or the Mind's Eye. Just so that you see through your mind's eye, always. In that sense, Mindscape is the representational map of his or her Mind's eye. One's desires, goals, and such things are also products of that Mind's eye's ways of mapping the life-world. Now, notice that mind's eye' is constantly engaged in busy activities during his or her waking hours of everyday life, as it is the controlling centers of every bodily movement, as simple as raising his hand to scratch his itch nose, putting one right leg ahead of his left leg, thinking a thought, conjuring up the image of the strange person he encountered in a subway car yesterday, or whatever else. When that busily engaged (non-stop day-in and day-out) mind's eye is put to sleep, suspending its usual activities, then the 'screen' of the mind's eyes goes blank, as does the computer screen when it is turned off or simply put into 'sleep mode'. The suspension of the Mind's eye enables one to enter into the state of Calm Mind (or Jeongshim 靜心), which is the necessary prior step to getting into the state of *myeongsang* (瞑想, I, for one, dislike using the term 'meditation' or 'meditative state' in my belief that these terms, commonly used in Western discourses on Zen). Then, what is so unique about the state of *myeongsang*? It is not just a state of mind, but an existential state of mood or milieu, his or her *whole being* enters into. The preceding sentence implies that we modern men and women are not living a life of an integrated whole being, many of his or her sensory organs shut off, therefore unable to sensuously respond to the environing world that is full of rich repertoire of potential interactions, and the culprit for such impoverishment was none other than his or her mind, crowded with arbitrary categorical matrices of knowledge, which are the active agents of obstruction, just as some installed software programs actively prevent some other programs to function as programmed and thus requiring a frequent re-configuration of the computer environments.

At last, in that state of *myeongsang*, mind's eye shut off, it's mindscape not erased but merely suspended, put to sleep; then, only then, even the sensory organ of the eyes begin to act as the **sensory organ** that it is, processing as a brute-force agency from the outside, merely impacting upon the optical nerves of the eyes. Furthermore, now finally, all other sensory organs, --such as each square millimeter of the skins that cover our body, the nose, the ears, the hairs on our heads and in other parts of our body as antennas, open up and interact with all invisible but nevertheless sensuous forces (some in the form of voices, shapes or whatever else kinds) in the world. In that state of *myeongsang*, the Artist, as a sensuous Being, is responding to all the rich spectra of colors, voices, smells and other forces of Natural Environment impacting upon his fully awakened Body, fully integrated with his Mind, therefore fully awoke in every cell of his body; the Artist's painting-acts or gestural movements with his fingers, hand and arms are not guided by his mind, willfully or intentionally. They just occur in response to and in natural interaction with his internal chi-energy forces in cosmic dance with the forces from outside his body. Therefore, it is not correct to call Kim Tschoonsoo's painting 'Action' Painting, for his painting-act is not intended Acting, guided by his mind's controlling nerve centers. They are ***muwui(無爲)acts***, rather than ***yinwui(人爲)acts*** of painting. Now, finally, we are perhaps ready to give a more precise definition to what he does as a painter in the following way: Kim Tschunsoo dances with his hands and fingers, applying paints and then scratching and some other similar such repertoire of movements in a dance of *'seu-seu-ro-chum'*. As a material being, all kinds of currents such as electric, magnetic, air, blood, water, hormonal fluids, and chi-energy circulating throughout our human body incessantly, without stopping, and much of such circulation is made possible through our breathing, in and out. In all different traditions of *myeongsang-hada*, whether in *Seon Buddhist* (禪佛敎), *Daoist* (道家), *Seon-ga(仙家)* tradition of Dan (丹), Yogic or Tantric traditions, it is through controlled breathing exercises that all the internal body-and-mind's states of configuration are managed and controlled. Through such exercises, one brings oneself to the state of *myeongsang* whereby one is finally capable of suspending, putting to sleep mode, all of his or her currently running mind's categorical matrices in complexly re-configured installation-fields; and, finally, at that state, one is, unconsciously, put into a direct contact with all sorts of other circulatory vibrations that fill the universe. Every object, whether it is a concrete building or a stone or a tree on a river bank, they all have its own characteristic vibratory wave length, just as every human being has his or her own characteristic finger-print like no one else's; in other words, it is possible to enter into the cosmic dance, wave to wave, consonant dance with similarly expansive wave-length, gather others capable of entering into the same consonance. A dance which has never been preprogrammed, never choreographed in any precise way, but the steps, gestures and movements coming out by themselves, as if they have been so induced by some external forces – that is what we already mentioned above, *'Seuseuro Chum'*. In that sense, this dance is **site-specfic** too, as the chi-energy configuration of the site at that moment has a lot to do with what kind of dance movements are coaxed out of the dancer. It is just in this way that Kim Tschunsoo dances with his fingers, hands and his entire body with the canvas on the canvas, its four squares, as his partner and as his dance floor. As a matter of fact, a Dance Professor at Seoul University of Art, **Kim Gee-yin** has made her name precisely with this particular kind of dance, which she named it *'Seuseuro Chum'*.(I must add that this Seuseuro Chum is actually a co-creation between her Chi-energy Exercise Teacher, Kim Kyeong-hoon and herself.)

This kind of dance is profoundly healing of one's body and mind, as the chi-energy-induced movements untangle whatever irregular circulatory knots in her body and mind and usher out of her system on the shoulders of some outgoing waves into the air [and thence to the universe]. One might compare it to an acupuncturist or to a masseur to open the blocked circuitry in one's body; but one can use dance movements, instead, to achieve the same thing. No wonder that body works (whether they the Western kinds of Rolfing, Alexander Technique, Lowen's Bioenergetics or Haller Methods or Feldenkreis, or the Eastern kinds of Seon Meditation, Danjeon-Hoheup), they are now attracting wide attention as an alternative methods of healing, alternative to the institutionalized Western Medicinal Technology.

As a modern men and women, living in the 21st Century, we've all forgotten, out natural ability that we were all born with, perhaps atrophied from non-use, to see, to hear or feel the palpable, real, actual, vibrations of chi-energy waves continuously impacting on us, our body. It is well known that we cannot hear unless the sound waves belong to a certain spectra of wave length, width, or frequency. So, just because we cannot hear or see or feel, it doesn't mean that there're not things and forces out there for us to respond to and enter into a cosmic dance. Indeed, the Masters of Northeast Asian **Suhaeng(修行),** of which **'Seon-hada'** (which means to do Seon-meditation) is just one among other such Suhaeng tradition, tell his or her disciples to listen to Qi-energy vibrations, as the Qi-waves impact on certain point of his body in a controlled breathing exercises; the Master will also tell the disciples to learn to see, not through the eyes that enables him to see visible things, but the eyes as just another sensory (optical) nerve endings that process impacting light waves from outside. (Indeed, it was none other than Albert Einstein himself who first showed that light waves physically impact on certain matters and create photo-electric effects that can be scientifically detected in experiments.) The master will also tell them to smell and to feel (tactilely) the impinging Qi-waves on the sensory nerve ending of their noses and each different part of the skin of his body.

To the novice or to the uninitiated, the Master's instruction would sound ludicrous, plain madness, in fact. Yet, it is precisely the very reason why *'Suhaeng'*, or *'Myeongsang-hada'* has become such an important issue of our Age, as its importance is indicated by this simple fact – that there are more Meditation Centers or Yoga Studios in most major European or North American Cities like New York, Paris, Berlin or London, outnumbering the popular and fashionable chain stores of Starbucks or Coffee Beans. Once you calmed your mind, and the state of 'myeongsang' occurred to you (and here please notice that I wrote that it occurred to you rather than saying that you got into that state); then, you have rediscovered the *Wholesome Existential Being that you are*, every single cell in your entire body fully awake and functioning in full synchrony with the rest of 'You', thus enabling you to recover your ability to converse with the more-than-human cosmos, to renew reciprocity with the surrounding powers of earth and sky, to invoke kinship even those entities which, to the civilized mind, are utterly insentient and inert. In just in that way, Kim Tschunsoo is a Suhaeng-ja (修行者) before he is an Artist, is capable of communing with the Mountain Peaks, Mountain Valleys, the trees, the forests, the streams, the boulders, the stones, the insects, the birds and occasional human climbers and other animals; but the mode of communing, in full reciprocity, is not to be in terms of the pre-established representational images, semiotic symbols or such stuff of the Mind, as was done before he was a *Suhaengja*. His communion is now at the most primordial way, being to being, matter to matter, wave packets to wave packets. Kim's covering of the square field of his canvas with paints, using nothing but his fingers, finger nails, hands, arms and such things, is not an Intentional Act of so composing in just such a way as the finished work appears to the gallery-goers.

According to Alexander Lowen's (creatively developing Wilhelm Reich's insights) theory of Bio-energetic Psychotherapy, founded upon the fundamental premise of the energetic underpinnings of both body and mind; a person is basically his or her body, all life's experiences are ultimately body experience. The body's expressions, postures, patterns of muscular holding, and energetic integrity (blocks, splits, fragmentation, etc.) tell the story of a person's emotional history. Reich-Lowen's understanding of human body comes perilously close to Ancient Northeast Asian understanding of human body. In Ancient Korean Language, as it is in modern Korean, human body is referred to as 'Mohm' (몸) which has to be clearly distinguished from '*Yukche*(肉體)' or '*Shinche*(身體)', whose literal meaning should be given as 'meat machine'. Mohm, in contrast, is a derivation from 'Muiyohm'(뮈욤) which means the System of Qi-energy Management inside his or her body. As a system of qi-energy-circulation management, it deals with inflow as well as the outflow of qi-energies and thus it enables the human body to interact with the surrounding environment. It is also thus that, according to Reich, emotional memories are stored in different body parts which his body-oriented psychotherapy untangles in order to heal his patients' spiritual or psychological or emotional unbalance.

Kim Tschunsoo, the Suhaeng-ja sees, smells, hears, while climbing mountain peaks and walking along the valleys, all kinds of different things he encounter, not just with eyes, nose or ears; but, he'd be interacting with all those things, resulting in a qi-perceptual experiences, which is stored in his body parts and then they are poured out, as it were, in a voluntary series of qi-induced his bodily-gestural movements with his fingers and hands and arms among other things. Because it is his qi-induced-perceptual experience, not through his conscious mind's eye, his painting appears to be all-over, as qi-energy-induced perceptual and expressive experiences can only be all-over and at the same time voluntary. No one consciously directed his fingers to scratch and draw and apply paints in just that seeming composition, so intended. As such, Kim's is an *Art of Feeling* rather than that of concepts and representations.

Of all human body parts, his or her fingers are the most sensitive instrument, at least on the par or possibly superior to tongue. In making love, man or woman uses his or her fingers and tongues to probe, feel, and give pleasure to one another. You don't feel with your mind, but with your heart, they say. But, perhaps, it should be said that you feel with your fingers. In talking about *feeling*, there're at least two seemingly different meanings to the same English word: for example, when one says that she feels sad and when one says she used her fingers to feel the hardness of her husband's muscular chest. Presumably, the first kind of feeling is what is done with her 'heart'. Now, however, we can say that the two kinds of feeling are not actually distinct ones; we just didn't know enough about human brain until now, although Spinoza already had a quite advanced philosophical theory of human emotion and feeling, without the benefit of the scientific discoveries in Brain Sciences in recent decades. (Well, that's why Spinoza is such a genius, being cable of seeing far beyond what was available in his historical time.) Let me explain:

Human emotions are triggered by emotion-competent objects outside; however, what triggers human feelings, according to Spinoza and modern Brain Scientists, is not from the outside (external) sources but from deeply within his or her body, feeling being the direct expression of his or her body states at that precise time of this feeling. But, of course, that particular state of body might have been triggered by having that emotion, triggered by an external emotion-competent source (an object or an event). Once in that mood (or feeling), then it might change his or her vision (seeing) of the outside object(s) in turn. It is important, however, to keep in mind that feeling is not a perceptual process mediated by any sort of visual perception first. This point can be brought home by pointing out that even in pitch black darkness whereby human figures cannot be seen visually, a human subject can feel (instinctively) that the suddenly appeared a dark figure (of a man or woman) is a hostile presence or not. Visual perception takes place through the sensory organ of the eyes alone, so to speak, whereas *feeling* takes place with the entire body *as a whole* responding, thereby instantaneously configuring his or her body in that particular way and thus having that particular feeling as a direct expression of that body state (in that particular body configuration).   Now, we see what Kim does in terms of Spinoza's notions of emotion and feeling, having origin deeply within human body states, even from a bare minimum sketch of his theory above.

Kim is in love with Korean Mountains and Valleys. He hikes and climbs any and each mountain in South Korea in order to commune, feeling the very geological contours and configurations of the mountain region, smelling and responding to the tactile feelings of the particular milieu each mountain peak and valley configure for itself. Not only with his eyes but more importantly with his body, he feels the different things he encounter during his sojourns, sometimes prolonged, in the mountain areas. Therefore, it is not the visual representation of what he saw with his eyes; rather, it is what he felt at each steps he took through the peaks and the valleys, and those feelings, as the records of his body states at each such feeling-instance (or event) are stored in his very body parts, in his finger-tips, in his legs, in his other muscular parts of his body. Therefore, it is right that he uses his fingers to paint, for the history of his feelings during his mountain climbs cannot be represented with his brush and ink, as they are not the instruments of FEELING. Feelings can only be felt with one's fingers and then indirectly with his heart, or tongue; as such this kind of feelings cannot be imparted or conferred onto the canvas with the usual brushes or any other such means.

Kim's Painting-Acts are self-healing, as he says himself. He chose to paint this way with his fingers and using only this particular hue of Blue; it is noteworthy that he was led to them, to paint with his fingers and use only this hue of Blue. He felt comfortable, in consonance with the invisible but nevertheless materially present light spectrum of that particular color, hence in working with this color, he is healing himself. We talked about *Seuseuro Chum* above, but there is also *Seuseuro Painting* in which even the selection of a color is done unconsciously, merely guided by his finger or fingers to that particular shade of color and not to others. In some such a way, Kim is a *Seuseuro Painter*.

End

www.ingramcontent.com/pod-product-compliance
Lightning Source LLC
Chambersburg PA
CBHW080648180526

45168CB00008B/3345